INSTINCTIVE SHOOTING

INSTINCTIVE SHOOTING

A Step-by-Step Guide to Better Bowhunting

by G. Fred Asbell

Library of Congress Catalog Number: 87-073505
ISBN: 936531-05-3

Third Printing,

Dedication

This is for my pop and my mother, Dwight and Georgia Asbell. Considering my early years, they could never have imagined this — a book. Mrs. Wilson, my English teacher, would be the only one more surprised.

Contents

Part II

G. Fred Asbell

Opening

Shooting a bow and arrow is one of the real joys of life for me. It has been that way almost from the very first. As a youngster I was obsessed with cowboys and Indians...mostly. Indians actually...perhaps my love of the bow is a natural outgrowth of that childhood play. I'm sure some pipe-smoking, bespectacled psychiatrist could figure it all out. I only know that it's what I like to do, and that few other things are as important.

There are times when nothing in the world is as relaxing and as enjoyable for me as wandering through the woods and across the fields, shooting arrows at leaves and clods of dirt...whatever strikes my fancy and seems like a decent test of my skills. It is not unusual for me to shoot several hundred arrows a day, each day, when I'm on a hunting trip. For several years I've bear hunted each spring in southern Colorado with Gary Bohochik out of Salida. Usually I'm in camp by myself. At that time of year the days are long and, after the early morning frost burns off, the days are sunny and warm. Often I'll shoot for four or five hours each day, waiting for the evening hunt. Part of it is keeping my eye for the hunt, but the majority of it is simply that I thoroughly enjoy shooting a bow and arrow and can amuse myself for hours doing it.

But, even though I enjoy simply shooting a bow, and in the '60's shot a great deal of field archery, competitive archery has never had much appeal to me. It's a fine thing, if you like it. But, I've found that the things you must do, the system you must develop to beat some other guy's score has very little place in the field. And as near as I can tell, in most cases it is a hindrance to the average bowhunter.

The more I shoot a bow and arrow, and the more I hunt, the clearer it becomes to me that shooting a bow for sheer fun and for hunting is a different kettle of fish. Instinctive shooting is made to order for such things...sights and releases and such are not. Sights and releases and such seem such an agonizing affair to most shooters, and I often wonder how many of them are having fun...but that too is another kettle of fish.

My interest has been in shooting a bow for fun and for bowhunting. And for that reason you'll not find much talk in here about helping your score or telling you how to beat some other guy. This book is about shooting a hunting bow...from cover to cover. Instinctive shooting does not work well for the repetitive style of competition. The concentration required for instinctive shooting is intense. To bring that sort of intense concentration to the competitive shooting line for shot after shot is very difficult. Some manage it...but they are the exceptions. So, if your intentions are to read this book and then go to an archery tournament and try it out, you'll probably be somewhat disappointed.

You will hear, and I suppose I agree, that...the **basics** of bowshooting are the same...whether you are shooting at an animal, a clod of dirt, or a paper target. It's hard to grasp that sometimes when I watch some fellow with an overdraw cam bow shooting with a sight, a string peep, a two-foot stabilizer, and a mechanical release. It's hard to realize that we really are involved in the same general sport. It's a long trip back to where he and I have something basic in our shooting in common. It's sort of like comparing benchrest rifle shooting with squirrel hunting. We both go through the draw, the anchor, the aiming, and the release....or is it the draw, the aiming, the anchor, and the release...I know that, but...Anyway, we are, in general, basically the same. Much the same as a robotic and a man, each picking their nose, are the same. We have become so stilted...so mechanized...that we really almost don't have a common ground anymore. How sad.

Everything in this book will seem to be about shooting recurve bows. In most instances I could have said "longbow or recurve" instead of just "recurve" throughout this book (which would get very tiresome). Basically there are few real differences in the two...but there are some. They are mostly in the area of shooting technique, and to a lesser degree in the area of bow setup. I think I know an awful lot more about recurves than I do about longbows. And it is important to me that I talk only about what I know well, and not try to pump you all full of theory. I've shot recurves for over 25 years, and longbows for, maybe, only three years. I make my living building bows...recurve bows, for many years, and only recently we've begun making longbows. So, I guess I don't consider myself knowledgable enough to advise anyone in the use of longbows. I really don't feel that I know the little tricks and nuances that separate a longbow shooter from a guy with a longbow. But I am confident that most of the things I'll talk about in a recurve are applicable in a longbow.

As you read through the whys and wherefores and how-tos of instinctive shooting it may seem that I'm repeating myself from time to time. And, I guess, I sort-of do that...it's hard not to do that with instinctive shooting. Everything in instinctive shooting is tied together. You can't separate the bow from the mind. The drawing of the bow, the concentration, the aiming...all become a single thing, a single action. I found it is nearly impossible to talk about the individual steps and needs in instinctive shooting without telling you how it all ties together. You'll see what I mean as you progress with instinctive shooting.

Enough. You only learn instinctive shooting by doing it...and doing it...and doing it. It is time to begin...

1

The author's hunting companion, Bob Pitt.

The Traditional Revolution

It would be hard to write a book about shooting a bow by the instinctive method without first talking a little about the need for it and how we got there. I mean, let's face it, less than 10 years ago a national convention of instinctive bowshooters would have been cancelled for lack of interest. That's not the case today.

Does that mean that there is a whole new interest in instinctive shooting? Yes. But it isn't just instinctive bow shooting per se. The traditional equipment revolution has regenerated instinctive bow shooting. They are both tied very closely together. Instinctive shooting almost disappeared with the appearance of the compound bow...it didn't have to be that way, but it happened. The compound bow can be shot instinctively, but it seems to lend itself, for a whole pile of reasons, to shooting with a bowsight. We'll talk more about that later. But, first...because instinctive shooting and traditional equipment are so closely associated...maybe before we get into *how* to shoot a bow we ought to spend a little time talking about the traditional equipment revolution that's underway across the country.

Being an old stick-in-the-mud conservative, I have a natural aversion to the word "revolution." But I think it's probably the best word to describe what's going on. Certainly there's no violence associated

with it and there's no placard-carrying masses, but there is definitely a strong movement that is a radical departure from the direction we have been led...a revolt against something. And I think that is an interesting aspect of this movement to note. It is perhaps as much a revolt **against** something as it is a movement **to** something different. Which is always an interesting aspect of change...there is something to be read in the tea leaves, there is a message in every revolution...be it a national uprising, or a revolt by your teenage daughter against your curfew rules.

A few years ago when 95 percent of the bowhunters in this country were shooting modern equipment...which most seem to feel demands the use of complicated aiming systems...there would have been little need for a book about instinctive shooting. I don't know what the numbers are...that is, how many bowhunters are shooting recurves and longbows these days. But, I know that the numbers are many times higher than they were a few short years ago...and there can be no question that they are increasing daily.

When we at Bighorn Bowhunting Company began building recurve bows in the mid-'70s (which is another story), people really thought we were crazy. They came to look at our wares like you'd go to a museum. "Look, honey, this is the kind of bow

15

I used to shoot...isn't that something?" I remember being at the Colorado Bowhunters Association summer jamboree in those early years and being one of eight bowhunters there who was shooting a recurve...and there were about 1,000 shooters in attendance.

Today it's much different here in Colorado. Again, I have no idea what the exact number might be, but I believe that maybe 35 percent of the 2,000 people in attendance at last year's jamboree were shooting either recurves or longbows. That's an unbelievable turnaround in only a few years. States like Montana, Oregon, Washington, Indiana, Ohio and Michigan...and I've probably left out others...have experienced a similar major swing toward traditional equipment. A couple of those states could be over 50 percent traditional equipment.

Traditional bowhunting equipment is popping out of the woodwork. Suddenly, recurves are back and longbows are becoming more and more evident. Everywhere you look this guy or that guy is dragging his old recurve out from under the bed and going to the woods with it. Many of yesterday's dyed-in-the-wool compound shooters are spending their evenings perusing catalogues from the myriad of custom bow manufacturers that have sprung up overnight. Going back to traditional equipment seems to be the thing to do.

Some would argue that "going back" is not the correct terminology, but rather that "stepping up to the challenge" better fits the mood. I think there is some truth to that. While recurves and longbows came before compounds, and many bowhunters shot them before they picked up the compound, it does not automatically follow that returning to a recurve is regression, a step backward. I think it could more accurately be looked at as a conscious decision to come at bowhunting from a different angle...to put more personal effort into the sport. The wording of the thing...whether you are "going back" or "stepping up"...is unimportant, I guess. Semantics are only focal points for arguments anyway. **You** get to decide whether you are retreating or going forward...whatever others call it, you make up your own mind.

What's happening? Why are people switching to traditional equipment? I would offer that the reasons are as numerous as are those who have changed. Each person has, more or less, a specific personal reason for switching to traditional equipment. But generally speaking, I would place the reasons into five categories:

1. Challenge
2. Tradition
3. Backlash reaction
4. Peer pressure
5. Improved hunting

"Recurves are back..."

Challenge—It seems to me that very often the decision to go to traditional bowhunting equipment arrives with experience...as an added challenge. And I don't mean a challenge like, "I'll bet you can't shoot an elk with a recurve"...that's a different kind of challenge. I see this challenge as being very much like the decision to be a trophy hunter. Having been successful at shooting "just" deer for several seasons, the hunter decides that next year he's going to hold out for a "big" deer...perhaps a Pope & Younger. The decision to switch to equipment that requires more personal involvement, more effort, is very similar to that decision to "switch" to hunting trophy animals instead of the easier ones. And very often the switch to trophy hunting and the switch to traditional equipment come at almost the same time in a hunter's development cycle. "Next year I'm gonna hunt with a recurve." It's an extra, additional challenge, truly a "step up."

Tradition—For many people the recurve is the traditional bowhunting weapon, and when they visualize a bowhunter it's with one of those weapons in his hand. I guess I'd fall into that category myself. The people in this group are often those who have always shot recurves and have no interest in ever changing. Even though the compound has been around for a long time now, I've personally never gotten used to seeing them in a success picture. Hunting with a bow and arrow is many things to me, not the least of which is a ritualized immersion into yesterday, and yesterday's values when it was understood that nothing came without working for it, and bow shooting and bowhunting ability were something that a man worked hard and long to attain. Like many others, I don't shoot traditional equipment because I think it's better (even though it may be)—or because it's more challenging (it is)—I do it because it's just how I think you're "supposed" to do it. It's as basic as that. It's like wood arrows...I don't shoot wood arrows because I think they're better, I shoot them because I **like** wood arrows...I like the **idea** of wood arrows. It has very little to do with logic...logic isn't necessary when it's what you want to do and how it must be for you.

Backlash Reaction—This group is growing faster than any, I think. I see them as being in two groups.

Group A has sprung up almost as a defiant reaction, perhaps a counter response, to the growing proliferation of technology in modern archery equipment. This is a philosophical break with today's ideas of what constitutes bowhunting equipment. Items like the compound crossbow, lighted sights, overdraws, releases, etc. have pushed these people over the edge. The more technology invades bowhunting, the larger this group becomes. It's a sort of, "I've had it...that's enough...this isn't bowhunting anymore" response. Group B is somewhat different. While there often is a philosophical break with modern equipment, as in Group A, there is a stronger desire to escape the complexities of modern equipment...a desire to get back to a simpler form of bow shooting and bowhunting.

Peer Pressure—One of the strongest human responses...what others are doing...has brought innumerable bowhunters to the ranks of traditional archery. It was a major factor in the rush to the compound bow...it is now a major factor in the migration to traditional equipment. If the two guys you bowhunt with each year switch to a recurve, there is a very good chance you'll do the same. And particularly if they are being successful and seem to be having a better time than you are. Look around. A major percentage of the really successful, really experienced bowhunters are hunting with recurve bows. And that number gets bigger and bigger with each passing bow season. And that number has a strong effect on causing others to try their hand at this traditional bow stuff. We're all affected by it.

Improved Hunting—This one attracts a few bowhunters, but surprisingly it isn't a major reason why people decide to **try** traditional equipment. It is a major reason why us old "wouldn't change for nothing" guys stick with it, but I am reasonably sure that very few bowhunters actually believe they'll do better with a recurve or a longbow. But...while people change to traditional equipment for all of the preceding reasons...

The Fact That Traditional Bows Work So Perfectly For Bowhunting Is The Major Reason Why Bowhunters Stay With Them.

So, while improved hunting doesn't actually **attract** many, it is one of the key reasons for the continued success of traditional equipment. I think most new traditional bowhunters are amazed, actually shocked, that this thing really does work...it really does kill animals...it really can be shot well.

Why does it work so well? I think the answer lies in its simplicity. Toss in the instinctive shooting method and shooting a bow and arrow couldn't get any simpler. The bow itself is pretty straightforward and simple...a curved stick and a string. Put your arrow there on the string...pretty close to center...and then draw it back to your cheek and turn it loose. 'Course, you do need to be a bit more technical about it than that...put a nock point on the string, find some arrows that match the bow and some protection for the fingers and the arm...and then go for it. It's not a lot more complicated than that. For many of today's bowhunters, the simplicity of a recurve has a lot of appeal.

Recurve bows and longbows are very simple. In another chapter, we'll cover how to set up a recurve bow. For the moment let's just say that there is almost nothing that can go wrong with a recurve, short of busting it into two pieces. Once tuned properly, it is likely that you'll not need to mess with a recurve again until you wear it out. Oh, if you put a new string on it, you'll have to adjust the brace height and put a new nock point on it...which should take about 15 minutes.

In all honesty I don't think I could stand going to the woods with a bow that could suddenly go out of adjustment on me...and that there would be a chance that I'd not be able to get it back into adjustment. I know nothing about the ills of compound bows, but it seems to me that in every hunting camp I've been in, that the majority of the people I've seen hunting with compounds are either in the process of trying to tune theirs, about to tune them, or complaining that theirs is out of tune. They remind me of the guys with go-karts back in the '60s..."It's not running right...usually it'll run a lot faster than this. I readjusted that carburetor awhile ago, but it's still not right." Tinker, tinker...worry, worry. Every man to his own, I guess...but I don't understand how guys can walk into the woods with something so sensitive that it can get out of adjustment just because it wants to aggravate you.

Most of us are familiar with horror stories about broken wires and widgets and bowstrings which couldn't be fixed until the end of a hunt...many have seen too many broken wheel bows, lying crippled and out of commission like the wreckage of a shot-down helicopter with its workings scattered across the ground. A couple of years ago, while hunting mule deer out of Jay Verzuh's camp on Colorado's Pinon Mesa, a fellow's bowstring on his compound was cut in the melee of loading gear and bowhunters into pickup trucks in the dark on opening morning. There was nothing he could do. It could not be put back together again in anything less than several hours, he claimed. I thought he was going to cry...opening morning of a guided hunt and a broken bowstring puts you out of commission. Ridiculous! It took two or three guys and a couple of helpers the bigger part of one whole day to get that compound bow back together again.

Recurve bows are easier to shoot under hunting conditions. They draw and shoot much smoother and quieter than does a compound. They can be shot from almost any sort of position you might find yourself in...and they can be shot quickly without concern for the two dozen things that many compound shooters put themselves through before they shoot. Colorado bowhunter Marv Clyncke tells a story about how he and Doug Beck, both recurve shooters, each dropped running javelina in Arizona this past year. There were two other fellows armed with 85-pound overdraw compounds along who could not believe that Marv and Doug could draw and shoot their bows that quickly—And how in hell could they possibly have hit the javelina, even though both shots had been made at about 10-15 feet? Marv said that all through the rest of the hunt the two fellows kept trying to jerk their bows to full draw, look through their peep and trigger their releases without the arrow ending up off their overdraw, or without shooting themselves in the foot or the hand, but they never were able to accomplish it. Like he said, "You sure hate to laugh at a guy, but you couldn't believe how funny it was to watch them."

Many bowhunters are finding that the stories they've heard about how slow recurve bows shoot are just that...stories. Many of today's top-of-the-line custom recurves actually shoot faster than a compound. Lots of people don't realize that. Now...before all the overdraw, cam-bow owners start screaming, the fastest compounds on the market will still shoot faster than will a recurve. But the difference is slight. The average compound and the average better-built recurve are about the same. So...many people are finding that they are not being penalized by shooting traditional equipment, and that with the other advantages inherent in traditional equipment, there isn't any reason to stick with the more complex system.

But I guess the thing I hear the most, the statement I hear more than any other from those who have changed from a compound to a recurve, is simply, "This is more fun." Most of them go on to say that shooting and practicing is something they are really enjoying again. Many say that they hadn't realized it, but shooting a bow had gotten so it wasn't any fun anymore, and that going back to the recurve was sort of like rediscovering bowhunting again.

2

"...No sights or aiming devices (are) used..."

What is Instinctive Shooting . . .and how does it work?

My own definition of instinctive shooting would go something like this: **Instinctive shooting is shooting a bow using only the abilities of eye, body coordination and instinctive memory.** And then I would go on to say: **It is shooting an arrow where you are looking. It is looking at the target and shooting.**

There are no sights or aiming devices of any type used in instinctive shooting. No reference points, no marks on the sight window, no marks on the string...nothing. The point of the arrow is not used either.

How does it work then, you say? Well, let me explain a little more about it and I think it'll start to make sense to you. Here's the technique: You draw the bow to anchor, look only at the thing you wish to hit and release. What you are doing is looking...concentrating on what you want to hit...and simply allowing your hand and your eye to point the arrow in the proper place. And both the hand and the eye do it somewhat subconsciously in that they do not use anything for reference except "feel." Shooting a bow instinctively isn't much different than throwing a ball. It is hard to say just how to throw a ball into someone's outstretched hands 20 feet away. You don't say to yourself, "Those hands are 20 feet away, so I'll throw the ball like this." Of course you don't. You simply look at

what you are throwing at and cut loose...right? It's a "feel." The more you practice it, the better, the more accurate that "feel" becomes. You cast a fishing line in much the same manner. Looking at where you want your bait to hit, you simply allow your arm and your eye to instinctively decide how it happens. We sit in front of the television on weekend afternoons and watch a variety of college and pro quarterbacks perform nothing less than instinctive magic with a football. Without the aid of anything but his arm and his eye, the quarterback throws a football 50 yards downfield, over the heads of two defensive backs and into the arms of his teammate, who is running like a scalded dog. How can he do that without some sort of aiming device? It ain't possible...is it?

I'd be willing to bet that, even though it's been 20 years since I tried it, I could, right now, pick up a football and throw it within catching distance of a streaking neighborhood 12-year-old...and I'll bet you can, too.

It's not magic.

It's a skill each of us possesses. It's called hand-eye coordination. It's nothing more than the ability to make your hand and your eye coordinate...to make them work together. A Ping-Pong ball comes bouncing across the net toward you. You keep your eye on the ball and swing the paddle up to meet it, knocking it back across the net. That's hand-eye coordination. You don't need gadgets and devices to make it work...you just do it. Hand-eye coordination is what you're using when you throw a baseball, a football, a fishing lure or hit a ball. We accept the ability to do those things...really without thought. In fact, we actually find it funny if a friend or a wife **can't** do it. Right? And yet, shooting a bow and arrow instinctively utilizes exactly the same skills and the same hand-eye coordination and we think it's some sort of impossible, mystical talent that only the very gifted possess. Nothing could be further from the truth.

Photo by Fred and Dora Burris

3

"Instinctive shooting works better than any other method for bowhunting."

Why Instinctive Shooting?

Instinctive shooting **works better** than any other method for bowhunting. And that really is the answer to the question, "Why instinctive shooting?"

I have no doubts about it...it is the very best way, day in and day out, to shoot a hunting bow. And I don't just say that on a whim, or because it is some new something I tried last week that seemed to work. I say that based on 30 years of bow shooting, and perhaps more importantly, 30 years of bowhunting experience. And I say that based on 10 years of being in the bow business and talking daily with bowhunters from every part of the country, who do all kinds of bowhunting...tree stands, stalking, still-hunting...and who have all the same problems and experiences you and I have had. All of it continues to lead me back to the same place. Every day I become more convinced that instinctive shooting is, without question, the very best bow shooting method for a bowhunter.

And while the fact that instinctive shooting works better is the reason for doing it, it is probably best that I explain just why that is **because you must believe it, too.** You see, instinctive shooting can't really be done with any degree of success unless you believe in it...and that's not mumbo-jumbo. Instinctive shooting involves a lot of confidence and a lot of concentration, neither of which work well without your undivided belief in the undertaking.

Instinctive shooting is utter simplicity. Instinctive shooting is looking at what you want to hit, and then shooting, without any conscious attempt to calculate distance. It is not quite as easy as all that, in that it takes time to learn...but once learned it is unbelievably accurate.

First off, instinctive shooting works well because the bowhunter can draw and shoot without thinking about distance. Often in bowhunting it is necessary to make rapid decisions and shoot quickly. There is often no time to calculate yardage or wait for a more open shot. Imagine yourself, sitting in your tree stand...it's midmorning...you're a little drowsy. You hear a small sound and when you look around the buck is there. Where did it come from? You're sure there is only a moment before he hops the fence and is gone. Without any thought...except maybe whether the deer is going to discover you...you draw and shoot. At least that's how an instinctive shooter could do it. Could you do it? How many times have you found yourself in a similar situation? We often hear, "There wasn't time to shoot." And, of course, there are times when there **isn't** time to shoot. But time enough for an instinctive shooter to get off a shot and time enough for a guy with a rangefinder and a release and a peep and a sight to get it together are usually quite different things.

Here's another situation: Imagine this very nice buck walking straight toward you and just before he gets to where you want to take your shot, he turns right and disappears into the brush and you can hear him move off behind you. You wait and watch for awhile, but eventually you give him up and go back to watching the trail out in front of you. Ten minutes later you hear something and you turn your head slightly to look. There's the same buck, head down, sniffing the leaves, walking into a small opening all the way over to your left. The opening is small. But there is a clear view of the chest cavity. No time to calculate yardage...there is only a half-moment and the opportunity will be gone. If you have to think yardage and system, you're dead...and he's long gone.

How many times have you been in a tree stand and had a deer close, but never in just the right place for a shot? You follow it around behind your stand and you can't shoot. And then it turns and comes in close right at the base of the tree, but you can only see the hindquarters. Someplace in there the deer decides something is amiss and you can tell at any moment it's going to decide it's time to get out of there. You think about trying a shot as he steps around the tree, but he's alert and standing such that he'll see you the instant you move up there. He moves just a little forward...totally alerted now...and then he sort of whirls and takes a couple or three big, hurried, bounding leaps away from the tree and then stops, again partially hidden by brush. He looks around once more and you know he is all but gone. By squatting down as far as your safety rope will let you and turning your bow at a crazy angle, you can shoot under the big limb you've been resting your elbow on for the last two days. It's a clear shot from there. Could you make the shot? That sort of situation happens a thousand times a day in the deer woods...and mostly the deer escapes.

Another advantage of instinctive shooting that is closely associated with the ability to shoot quickly—without having to calculate yardage—is the ability to shoot your bow in any position. The bow can be upright or parallel to the ground—it does not matter with instinctive shooting. It matters a lot when you're shooting with a sight. The bowhunter must be capable of taking advantage of whatever opportunity the animal offers. Instinctive shooting is ideally suited to the flexibility of method the bowhunter needs.

Let me illustrate: This past fall I was slipping along the upper edge of a timbered ridge in Nebraska, looking for whitetails. I had stopped and was looking things over, about to move forward, when a flash of movement caught my eye almost straight ahead of me. In a moment a 10-pointer materialized out of the shadows 15 or 20 yards away and came walking, head down, toward me on a course that would take him by me at about five yards. The arrow had instinctively appeared on the string when I saw the first movement, so I was ready. About halfway to me, the buck turned somewhat to the right and, still not having seen me, began angling down the side of the ridge past me. As he passed...now below me...he was six, maybe 10 yards away. I slowly twisted my body at the waist as he passed, keeping my eyes on him, but not moving my feet (he'd have heard me instantly). I waited for a second until I thought he was far enough past that he might not see the movement and then I twisted as far as I could and with my bow parallel to the ground, pulled the arrow very slowly as far back as I could and just as the deer's eye caught my movement and his head jerked around toward me, I cut the arrow loose. He ran farther than I wanted him to...150 yards...but he'd seen me right there on top of him and had really gone out of there hard...otherwise I don't suppose he'd have gone half that far before he fell.

The point I'm trying to illustrate here is the total flexibility of instinctive shooting. First off, the bow was canted/turned parallel with the ground. Second, I doubt that I drew as much as 25 inches of arrow (my normal draw is about 29½ inches)...and third, I was eight inches or more from my normal anchor. Someplace down there close to the point of my shoulder is where I think I turned it loose. And a major point to consider is that this all took place in a total space of perhaps 15 to 25 seconds...maybe even as little as five or 10 seconds, I don't know. But I am sure that as the deer appeared and then came toward me there was no chance, nor time, to go through a variety of mental calculations and movements. I don't think anyone but an instinctive shooter is capable of making a shot like that. And the truth is, for an instinctive shooter it wasn't that big a deal.

Let's take it a step farther...a deer at that kind of distance is almost close enough to leap out and grab...and yet a majority of today's bowhunters with their complicated aiming and shooting systems could not make that shot. There's something wrong there, don't you think? Shooting a hunting bow has become such a stilted affair that a deer that happens on a bowhunter at point-blank range is pretty safe unless the guy is in an elevated stand and the deer appears where the hunter planned he would appear, and unless he gives the guy enough time, to get ready and draw. Many of today's bowhunters using today's shooting systems can only shoot when everything is "just so." We've become gunners who can only shoot under certain conditions. We're almost like robots. No flexibility...programmed for only certain tasks to be performed in only a certain order, with time required to check the range, hook up the old release, turn the peep just so, etc. And here I go again...hey, there's nothing wrong with shooting modern equipment, or using modern technique. But bowhunters are allowing it to dictate to them just how they're going to have to hunt. It baffles me that bowhunters don't see the limitations they've placed on themselves, the limits they've put on their success. It seems we've walked right by the simple basics of this wonderful sport of ours.

It seems to me that we are making shooting a bow a lot more complicated than it really is. Shooting a hunting bow is not difficult. It is not easy, in that it takes time and regular practice, but the basics are simple...in that simplicity lies one of its greatest rewards. And, I guess, I don't mean to be saying you're doing it wrong if you're doing it differently than I am...but, I'm pretty sure we're being led to believe the whole thing is more complicated than it really needs to be. And I am very sure that all the junk being hung on hunting bows is not necessary for zipping an arrow through a deer's chest at 20 yards. It is perhaps necessary for shooting two-inch groups at 35 yards on paper...but not for bowhunting. Let's face it, there are sights and there are sight megasystems...Lord!...what awful, preposterous monstrosities are sold under the guise of aiding the bowhunter. I looked at a combination arrowrest and bowsight the other day that was supposedly designed specifically for the bowhunter. There wasn't a way in hell some poor bowhunter was going to be able to use it in poor light, or when an animal was any closer than 50 yards, or with anything less than a perfectly set-up and executed blast off. I would have fallen on the ground in laughter if it wasn't for the sobering fact that some beginning bowhunter was more than likely going to come in there and buy the thing and believe he was now going to become a better bowhunter.

I have this theory...and I guess I might as well tell you about it right now. For a long time now I've been convinced that a big percentage of the guys with the complicated aiming systems shoot instinctively when an animal comes along anyway. How else can you explain how a guy who can shoot Ping-Pong ball-sized groups at 30 yards, all day long, can completely miss an elk at 11 yards? He would have to misjudge the yardage by at least 50 yards. I mean, shooting over an elk's back at 11 yards is putting the arrow as much as **three feet** too high. I think most just pull it back...never looking at their peep, post and what-have-you, and cut loose... instinctively, if you will...but without having practiced it, the effort is often in vain. Enough! I'll try to be more positive from now on and not talk negatively about other methods.

I'm personally sold on shooting a hunting bow instinctively. I think it works particularly well for bowhunting...and in the end, that is the only thing I'm concerned about.

4

Indiana bowhunter Bob Pitt—one of the best instinctive shooters the author has seen.

Shooting a Bow Well

It's very important that you learn to shoot a bow well. Fact is, it's an absolute necessity if you intend to seriously pursue hunting with a bow and arrow. How else but as a result of your shooting can you successfully kill an animal? It's the only way it gets done. If you can't hit anything, you might as well stay home and watch golf on TV. If you shoot badly, there's a good chance that you'll wound animals. "He shoots just good enough to hit most things and bad enough that he just wounds them" ...was a statement you'd hear back in my early days in Indiana that was considered particularly derogatory about a guy's ability. It was worse than calling a bowhunter a SOB. And, of course, if you're a poor shooter there's a better than even chance that you'll miss the biggest buck you'll ever see. There is also a very good chance that you'll get discouraged and eventually drop out of bowhunting. Which is what you should do if you continually wound animals. Need I say more? There are many reasons for you to work at being a good shot with your bow. Not the least is simply the personal pleasure derived from doing a thing well. The pleasure of sending an arrow directly dead center into the very leaf on that clump of weeds your imagination turned into a browsing bull or buck is not to be overlooked. Shooting a bow well is a good feeling. None of us gets to hunt as much as we'd like. Even for those with lots of money and few

obligations, the hunting season is pretty short. The rest of the year is spent preparing for that short time. More than with any other blood sport, you'll find your bowhunting successes dependent on the amount of off-season practice you've put in.

I can't for the life of me understand how bowhunters can put in hundreds, even thousands, of hours scouting and generally preparing themselves for the hunt...perhaps even spending piles of money...and then walk out there and not have any idea whether they'll be able to shoot within two feet of whatever comes along. Yet, every year in various hunting camps, I run into all kinds of bowhunters who shoot a bow so poorly that I feel like telling them they shouldn't be allowed in the woods. That's very sad to me. It is also very unnecessary. Shooting a bow well is a real pleasure...it is also a real necessity.

You'll find few consistently successful bowhunters who aren't at least average shots. If they are consistently successful year in and year out, you can bet money on their shooting decently. And when I say "shooting decently," I don't mean how they shoot at an archery lane or at a competitive shoot. Many good bowhunters do not shoot as well as others under such circumstances. That is not at all unusual. It is because shooting well competitively has very little to do with being able to shoot a hunting bow well. The equipment is different...the technique is very different...and the mental process for shooting competitively and for bowhunting is totally different.

However, let me add this, right here. I am not one of those people who believes that story about Ol' Joe. "Yeah, Ol' Joe there, he doesn't shoot worth a darn until something with hair on it walks by and then he never misses." I do not believe that story. Neither should you. In fact, everytime I hear it I feel like my intelligence has been insulted. How dumb can people think you are? I'm not going to say that "Ol' Joe" couldn't have, on occasion, made a decent shot on an animal. What I am saying is that I do not believe a guy who can't hit the ground with a quiver full of arrows is going to be suddenly transformed into a crack shot because an animal came by. It does not happen that way. I've heard the story about "Ol' Joe" often enough that it oughta be true, but I've not seen it yet. When I say a guy might not be able to shoot as well at an archery range, in front of others, I'm referring to the guy who doesn't shoot arrow after arrow into a tiny little wad...but he can group arrows somewhat and you can tell he knows how to shoot a bow. The guy who sprays arrows all over...one off the target, two into the backing and one into the target two places over...isn't going to do much better on animals. A man who can't shoot will not be transformed by being put into a hunting situation.

Shooting Ability Vs. Hunting Ability

You'll hear bowhunters say that being able to shoot well isn't important. And that knowing how to hunt is much more important than knowing how to shoot a bow. I would not agree with that. I **am** certain that learning to be a bowhunter is much, much more difficult than learning to shoot a bow...but it isn't more important. Actually, I would give them somewhat equal importance. And neither is worth a tinker's dam without the other. Being the best woodsman/bowhunter in the world is of absolutely no value if you cannot hit what you find. And certainly being able to hit dimes at 50 yards is useless if you don't know how to find something to hit. Most of us know bowhunters in each category: the great hunter who can't shoot for sour grapes and the league champion who knows absolutely nothing about bowhunting. Both have great skills...and yet each of them will end up with an unfilled tag each year.

You'll need both skills in varying degrees at various times. Shooting a bow well enough to kill animals consistently at 30 yards will, in fact, allow less hunting ability...as will enough hunting ability to permit your always getting to within 10 yards allow more success with less shooting ability.

My friend, Bob Pitt, is a good example of what bow shooting ability can do for you. Bob's Indiana trophy room is filled with big whitetails, mule deer and elk. There are also lesser quantities, but not smaller specimens of moose, caribou, bears and antelope. Bob is, for my money, as good a bowhunter...and as successful a bowhunter,...as there is in the woods. He is also one of the best shots with a hunting bow that I've ever seen. Bob shoots purely instinctive. He shoots recurves in the 60 to 65 pound range. A good part of Bob Pitt's phenomenal success lies in the fact that when he shoots an arrow at an animal, the hunt is generally over. His shooting ability plus his being an exceptional hunter allows him to consistently get himself into position to put a lot of good animals on the ground. He has it all. His ability and his experience in the woods seem to put him in the right spot an awful lot. But Bob claims that his shooting ability is his best skill. "Lots of guys get around big deer lots more than me...they just usually don't get them...that's the difference." It's rare when he misses a chance at an animal. Yes, he's cool under pressure...but I think it has a lot to do with the fact that he is **sure** he can't miss if the animal comes within range. He's a great shooter and he's confident about it. Bob Pitt is as close to being a bona fide bow and arrow "hit man" as you'll ever see.

Shooting a bow well is an asset. Without question it will make you a more successful bowhunter.

Photo by Fred and Dora Burris

5

The author at full draw. Note eye location and relationship
of arrow, bow hand and anchor.

Shooting Off the Shelf

Instinctive bow shooting starts with the arrow rest. Making that arrow go where you are looking begins with your arrow rest and with locating it as near the hand as possible. I call what I shoot and what I recommend, a "rug rest." I consider its use and its location critical to instinctive shooting.

Why is that? Well, let me review what we talked about in Chapter Two.

> Instinctive shooting is shooting a bow using only the abilities of eye, body coordination and instinctive memory.
>
> Oversimplified, it is shooting an arrow where you are looking. It is looking at a target and shooting. The ability to look at something and shoot the arrow to that spot is using the principle of hand-eye coordination.

Hand-eye coordination is the ability of your brain to pull together and coordinate the action of your hand with the vision of the eye. When you look at something with your eye, your hand has no difficulty reaching out and touching it. They are coordinated. Thus, in order for the principles of hand-eye coordination to become a factor in shooting an arrow, it is a necessity that the arrow be as near the hand as possible. Actually the arrow needs to be almost an extension of the hand...by

doing that we are sort of changing the principle from hand-eye coordination to arrow-eye coordination. Does that make sense? Read it again if it doesn't, because it is key to shooting instinctively.

We put the arrow as close to your hand as we possibly can, by getting the arrow rest as close to your hand as possible. Enter the rug rest..."shooting off the shelf" it is often called. By getting the arrow right down on the hand we are making the arrow an extension of the hand and the arm. We are putting it into the same plane as the arm, which is in the same plane as the hand when the bow is drawn and pointed.

For discussion purposes, there are two kinds of arrow rests. There are actually more like 2,000 of them but basically they all fall into one of two categories in my mind. There are shelf rests and there are elevated rests. A shelf rest is attached to— or is—the arrow shelf. Usually it is what I call a "rug rest," which is a hair-type plate somewhat resembling a very short crew cut. It could be a piece of leather or even a piece of felt. Vertical feather rests are generally lumped into this category, although they do hold the arrow a little high for my tastes.

An "elevated rest" is any of the many on the market which suspend the arrow above the shooter's hand (sometimes as much as three inches).

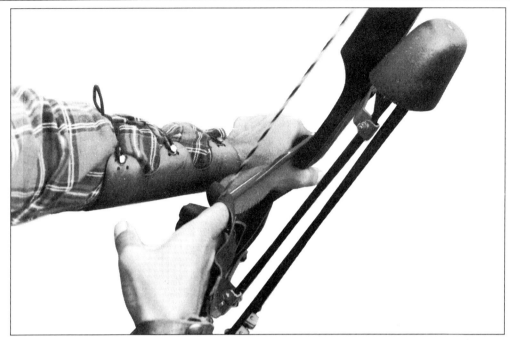

Here is a view showing the relationship between the rug rest, arrow, bow and bow hand.

A few attach to the arrow shelf, but most are attached to the side of the sight window. The fact that the elevated arrow rest is often close to the middle of the sight window, high above the shooter's hand, is the problem. With the arrow located in this position it is practically impossible to cant the bow and shoot it accurately.

Let me explain "canting the bow." "Canting" is the process of tilting or angling the bow to the right or left as it is being shot. The bow is canted as you shoot for a couple of reasons. The first, and primary reason, is that it brings the eye closer and more in line with the arrow as it is being drawn and shot. This is very important in instinctive shooting. You might also find yourself canting your bow to one side or the other in a given situation to prevent your bow limb hitting an obstacle (tree limbs, the ground, etc.) as you shoot. In the earlier story about the whitetail which I shot at very close range in Nebraska, I was forced to twist around at the waist and cant my bow drastically to get the shot off. Plus, the fact that the arrow was down near my hand

allowed me to shoot the deer by really just pointing my bow hand...without ever anchoring. In combination, the two...canting the bow and shooting off the shelf...are deadly. The combination of the two gives you more latitude and flexibility in your shooting than any other 10 things I'm aware of.

Another reason for canting the bow...and this was the original reason I began doing it...is to move the upper portion of the bow out of your line of vision. When we used to all shoot field archery back in the '60s, I found that on the longer shots if I canted the bow drastically, I had a clearer view of the target.

Canting the bow isn't as common as it used to be. I think that is for two reasons: first, there's the increased use of hunting sights which dictates that the bow must be held in a straight up and down position; and second, the use of elevated rests, which has a similar effect. Both negate the practice of canting the bow. Let me show you what I mean: Hold out your hand and make a fist, thumb up, as shown in Illustration #1. Your closed fist represents your hand wrapped around your bow handle, exactly as though you are shooting. The extended thumb represents an arrow on an elevated rest. With your arm fully extended as though you were shooting, aim your thumb (which is the arrow) at some object on the wall as in Illustration #1. Now you simulate canting your bow by rotating your hand as shown in Illustration #2. You are still supposedly aiming at the same spot on the wall, but as you can see, your arrow is nowhere near your target. If you shot like this, your arrow would miss its mark by a bunch. Now, again, using your closed fist at the same spot. Now the arrow is sitting on the top of your fist, as with a shelf rest (see Illustration #3). Do the same as before. Aim at

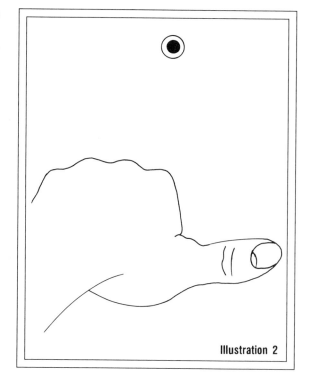

Illustration 2

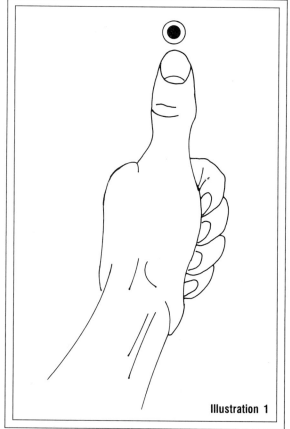

Illustration 1

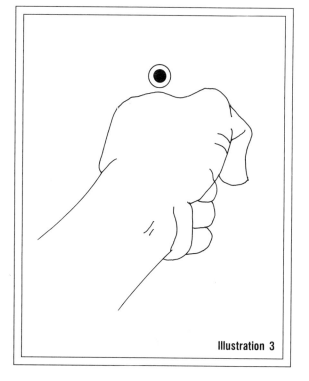

Illustration 3

the same spot and then cant the bow (your fist) to the right. Illustration #4 shows that the arrow is still pointing at the target. Hmmm! How about that? As you can see, canting your bow when you shoot off the arrow shelf doesn't change much of anything. With the arrow down near, or on, your hand, you are able to cant the bow left or right, and your arrow will still hit in about the same place. Interesting, huh?

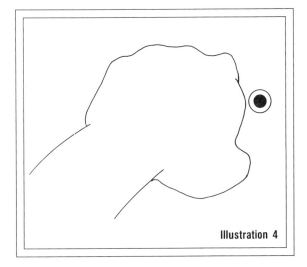

Illustration 4

The point I'd like to make is that getting the arrow down on your hand, where canting it right or left makes little difference in your shooting, can be a valuable asset to the bowhunter...even if he prefers shooting his bow upright most of the time. Personally, I cant my bow about the same amount most of the time, but I can shoot it from almost any angle when necessary.

And it isn't specifically that elevated rests are some great, complex obstacle that are going to keep you unsuccessful for the rest of your bowhunting life. With a great deal of today's modern equipment, I don't think you have any choice about whether you shoot off an elevated rest or not...but if you shoot traditional equipment you don't have to shoot them and if you shoot instinctively you **shouldn't** shoot them. The ability to shoot a bow quickly and simply is often paramount under hunting conditions. I personally would hate to think I **had** to hold my

bow straight up and down for every shot. A number of years ago I shot a bighorn ram while sitting flat on the ground with my bow canted almost level with the mountainside. I'd slid down the mountain on my back to stay below the animals' line of sight. When I was within range, I sat up and shot...while the sheep stared at me like they'd just seen a jack-in-the-box appear. It is important to my hunting to be able to cant my bow in whatever manner the situation dictates.

Perhaps it sounds as though I try to get myself into situations that require contortion-type shooting. It's not really true. I think it must be because I don't give any consideration to being in, or getting myself into, an exact stance or position before I can shoot. When I get close enough and the opportunity presents itself, I can shoot. I prefer shooting from my knees at an unsuspecting animal at under 15 yards. They do not always cooperate. Obviously, if you do all your hunting where you can plan on being able to always hold your bow in a prescribed manner, it isn't something you need to give a second thought. I've just never been able to always do everything "just so."

I tried shooting from an elevated rest a number of years ago. That was in the early '60s and everyone was saying you'd get better arrow flight, more speed, etc. I tried it and it didn't work for me. Besides the problem of canting the bow, everytime I tried to draw quickly the arrow fell off the rest and onto the arrow shelf (it sounded like someone dribbling a golf ball on a hardwood floor). The final straw was the high pitched screech my arrow made one cold morning as I drew it across the plastic rest. In about one half second I was completely alone in the woods. I admit I haven't tried it since.

At least a half dozen times each year I listen to sad tales of missed shots and screwed-up hunts because "my arrow rest broke." Most of the time, as the story goes, the hunter didn't realize it until too late. I always sympathize with these bowhunters...but I often consider asking them why they shoot those fragile pieces of wire, or those elaborate roller-bearing pieces of Detroit. I just don't know about us sometimes...we certainly have developed the talent for complicating our leisure

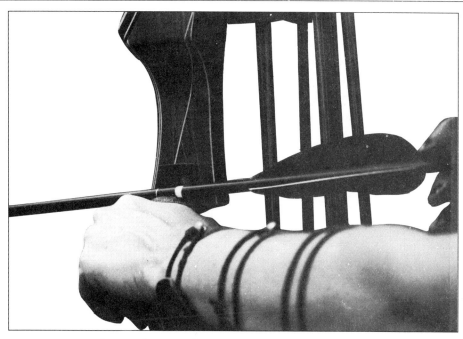

Correct placement of rug rest, arrow, bow and bow hand.

time in all sorts of new and ridiculous ways. It just never made any sense to me...putting all these obstacles between me and the animal I want...I've always been selfish that way. Shooting off the shelf is so simple, so uncomplicated...and your arrow rest will never, ever, break.

People ask how I ever get my arrows to shoot properly off a shelf rest. Most haven't tried it. But they've been told it won't work. Believe me, it will. I've heard the same stories. Stated simply, they aren't true. Actually, getting good arrow flight off a shelf has never been a problem for me, nor for anyone I know. I would point out that plastic vanes cannot be shot off a shelf, but then I've found that plastic vanes are difficult to shoot from even specially made arrow rests.

For someone who has never tried it, shooting off a shelf rest is somewhat different...but only in that it's so simple it's hard to believe. A good portion of the custom bows that are appearing today are, more or less, set up for shooting off the shelf—although not all of them. Production-built bows are another story, however...most are not set up for shooting off the shelf. High production equipment doesn't handle the traditional arrow shelf very well. I'm told that the front to back radius which we put in our bows—and then the lack of radius where the sight window joins the arrow rest—is an impossibility for high speed handle-shaping equipment. I assume that is true based on the fact that all the production bows I see are built with those horribly high contoured things that can only pass as the top of the grip or the bottom of the sight window, never as an arrow shelf. I guess they don't see them as serving a function, only separating the handle from the sight window.

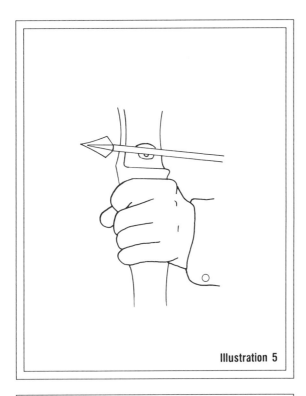

Illustration 5

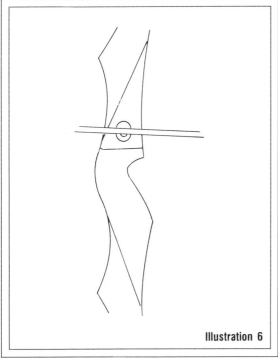

Illustration 6

Illustrations #5 and #6 show typical arrow and arrow shelf set-up. In my opinion, an arrow shelf should look like Illustrations #7 and #8. There is a minimum of arrow contact and the arrow is almost on the hand. Unfortunately, the only solution for many bows is often the use of a file or a saw. That is objectionable to some. You should check with the manufacturer of your bow and ask if altering the sight window will void the guarantee. They may be willing to do the alteration for you. I always figured if I couldn't fix the thing the way I wanted it, I might as well not have it anyway. Years ago, before I started building bows, when I bought a new bow the first thing I did was go buy a new file. But some bows simply cannot be fixed. In a case such as that, I'd try to get my elevated rest as close to my hand as I could. It's not as good...but it's better than nothing.

You might have to shoot a slightly higher nocking point off the shelf, but I've not found that to be a problem. Also I use a leather pressure plate that extends all the way across the sight window. I put a piece of paper match or a narrow piece of leather under it, directly above the deepest part of the grip. That becomes your pressure point, and by locating it above the deepest part of the grip you will minimize the effect of any handle torque that may take place.

Loss of arrow speed? Not to my eye. Although people who religiously keep track of such things say it's true, I can't see that it's significant with hunting weight arrows out of hunting bows. Because I intend to always shoot off the shelf, regardless of whether I lose two feet per second, I've done a minimum amount of chronographing. It wasn't all that scientifically done, actually. One test utilized a popular molded finger-type elevated rest. The material seemed to be almost rubber...at least similar to that material. It shot slower arrows than did the rug rest I normally use. I don't offer that as proof of anything...only evidence that elevated arrow rests are not necessarily going to give you a faster arrow. If there is a difference, I would suggest that it isn't significant...or maybe I should say it isn't **important** to me. To some, two feet per second is reason to swap bows, change styles, buy

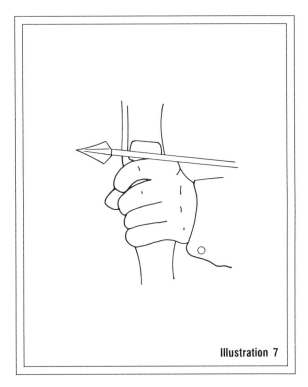

Illustration 7

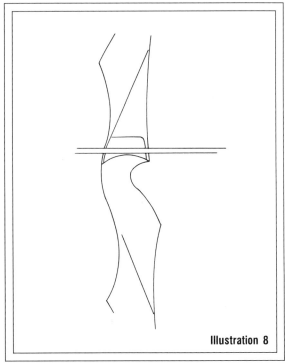

Illustration 8

another something, etc.

Shooting off the shelf is important because it greatly simplifies instinctive shooting. When the arrow is down on your hand, the arrow becomes part of a simplified pointing system. Basically, your arrow is pointed where your hand/arm is pointed. It will greatly improve your ability to shoot quickly and to shoot where your bow is pointing.

6

Author and trophy mule deer.

Learning to Shoot Instinctively

Learning to shoot a bow and arrow instinctively isn't a lot different than learning any other shooting technique, in that good results are a product of using a specific technique, repeatedly.

Does that surprise you? Did you think that instinctive shooting was simply jerking the bow halfway back, as fast as possible, and cutting one loose? Perhaps I've misled you. It may appear that a good instinctive shooter is pretty casual in his approach to shooting. It may also appear as though his technique is inconsistent and sloppy. I can see that you might believe that...particularly when I tell stories about not anchoring when I shoot. Those are not just "yank her back and let fly" shots. I guess they seem that way. But I knew exactly what I was doing...I expected to hit what I was shooting at.

The ability to do that sort of shooting is a product of form and practice. The fact that I have spent so much time shooting with a specific instinctive technique so familiarizes the instincts with a proper feel that one part of the shooting technique adjusts when another part does something different. For example, when the bow cannot be drawn fully, the bow arm automatically, without any conscious intervention, elevates the arrow properly. When the bow can only be drawn to, let us say, a location down around the point of the shoulder (six to eight inches below my normal anchor) the bow hand instinctively knows the proper adjustment to make.

Let me draw yet another comparison for you. When you first begin learning to play basketball, you are taught a specific technique. Hold the ball in two hands, elbows close in to the body, look straight over the top of the ball, and holding the left hand under the ball, use the right to push it toward the basket, etc. The game is taught to be played in front of the body...with all ball movement at eye level. Soon the player is taught to jump into the air as the shot is taken. If he becomes a good player, he will learn to shoot the ball from far above his eye level and sometimes in the form of a hook shot from high and back behind the head. With practice all these shots begin swishing through the net with regularity...even though he is no longer using the same basic form he originally learned. Watch professional basketball players as they warm up before a game. The shooting is loose and casual ...almost ho-hum sloppy. Sometimes they bank the ball off the backboard, sometimes they appear to be shooting completely off-balance, or hardly even looking at the basket. It's sometimes hard to imagine that their ability to just nonchalantly throw the ball into the air and have it go through the net is a product of form and practice. But had the pros not learned the basics to begin with, it is unlikely they'd be able to perform such artistry today. The same sort of ability begins to surface with instinctive shooting. Starting with a specific method...with a set way of doing something...continual practice will allow the hand and the eye to begin working together, regardless of the position of either. With practice, the eye adjusts automatically for the location of the hand (anchor)...as the anchor adjusts automatically for the eye (head position).

Remember this...no amount of personal ability in the world—and for that matter, no amount of hand-eye coordination—can make an arrow go to a place if it isn't pointed there. Instinctive shooting isn't some slapdash, half-baked method of making an arrow go where you want it to go. You learn casual instinctive shooting by first learning a basic technique of shooting. From that basic technique you can begin to develop almost uncanny skills, if you wish to practice hard.

Instinctive shooting is based on fairly rigid repetitive techniques that allow a form of memory to eventually begin directing the arrow to the target. In fact, it could be argued that instinctive shooting is more dependent on doing the same thing over and over again than are any of the other shooting styles. I don't think there can be any question that instinctive shooting requires more practice than any other shooting method. Or perhaps I should say that it takes more practice to learn...once the skill is ingrained, with the exception of maintaining the necessary strength, the skill requires very little maintenance. Stacy Groscup of West Virginia, who is one of the finest trick shooters I've seen, claims he rarely practices anymore. Stacy has shot a bow for many, many years. He told me that sometimes his first arrow in a demonstration is the first arrow he's shot in months. I don't recommend that. I offer it only as evidence that, once learned, instinctive shooting is like learning to shoot a basketball, or throw a baseball...the old muscles may get a little sore after a long layoff, but the basic skill never leaves.

No matter how you shoot a bow and arrow... instinctively, with a sight, point-of-aim, walking the string, or whatever...the basic, fundamental principles of bow shooting are the same. Those fundamental principles are the stance, the draw, the anchor, aiming and the release.

Each of these fundamental principles is important in learning to shoot instinctively. Their position and degree of importance to our style of shooting may be different than they are with other styles, but nevertheless, they are important.

With form and practice comes understanding of the workings of shooting a bow and arrow. Once you begin to understand the whys and wherefores of your shooting, you are well on your way to good shooting. I have always maintained that it is impossible to be a consistently good shot until you understand why you miss—and why you hit. Without that knowledge, you are playing in the dark, relegated to having "good days" and "bad days" and being unable to control either.

Throughout this chapter all my instructions relate to a right-handed shooter. Obviously, if you're a lefty, you'll have to reverse my directions.

The Stance

The "standard archery stance" is the most popular with shooters: left side toward the target, feet parallel and spaced comfortably, head turned 90 degrees with the chin touching, or almost touching, the left shoulder. The open or oblique stance is also popular. It is similar to the standard stance except the right foot is placed slightly forward of the left and the left foot is pivoted slightly toward the target. This opens the form somewhat, giving a little more body clearance and allowing a less strained address of the target. Either stance will work. But I think the open stance is probably better for instinctive shooting. It is more flexible than the standard stance and more closely approximates the body position bowhunters might find themselves in under hunting conditions. It is also a better body position for flexing the knees as the bow is drawn (which we will talk about in depth, near the end of the chapter). I personally use a version of the open stance. I stand about two-thirds facing the target, with my left foot, more or less, pointing toward my target. This stance works best for me.

The stance you choose is not critical. You should select one and stay with it through the learning

The standard stance.

The open or oblique stance.

stages of instinctive shooting. As a beginner you are establishing technique and laying the groundwork for your instinctive memory. And that is best learned through repetition of the same moves and the same style. Once you have established a shooting style and your instinctive abilities have taken root, then it is good to vary your stance as you practice anyway. I make a point of moving my body position with each shot. Later you can begin to try different feet and body positions. As your instinctive ability increases you'll find body stance becomes less and less important.

The Draw

The techniques for drawing the bow are most important. The mechanics include hand position on the bow, bow arm position, finger position on the string, the draw itself and head position during the draw. The draw, because it includes these key items, is the very heart of shooting instinctively...nay, **it is the very heart of all shooting**, any style.

Beginning with hand position on the bow, I recommend that you grip the bow with as near a straight wrist as possible. Breaking the wrist no more than just a slight amount will work against you for instinctive shooting. If you recall, in Chapter Five which discussed "Shooting Off the Shelf," we talked about getting the arrow as close to the hand as possible so that the arrow becomes an extension of the bow arm, and we showed drawings of why an elevated rest doesn't work well. Breaking your wrist, or setting the heel of your hand down on the bow, has almost the same effect as an elevated rest. As you can see in the accompanying illustration, with a broken wrist the arrow and the arm somewhat depart directions at the critical point. You'll find instinctive shooting simpler with a straighter wrist. Plus, with a broken wrist, the slightest change in hand pressure can cause tremendous variations in your shooting. I often see fellows who shoot bows which are too heavy for them, shooting with the heel of their hand down. Many of them also have their wrist broken inward

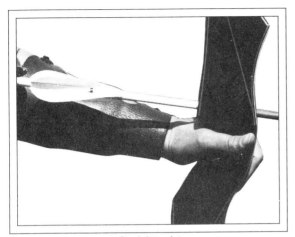

Straight wrist

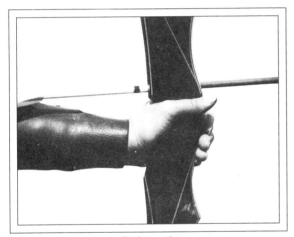

Broken wrist

The author's grip.

toward the center line of the bow and they just have an impossible time with torquing the bow. Certainly you're stronger with the heel of your hand down on the grip but it's practically impossible to shoot well this way. Do this: turn your left hand over so the palm is looking straight up at you. On most people there is a line in about the center of the heel of the hand. If there isn't one there on your hand, draw one there with a felt tip marker.

Now, with your bow in hand, with your fingers on the string (but not drawing it), slide your hand to the left on the grip until that center line (or mark) is to the left of the center of the bow. You should be able to determine center by glancing up at the sight window (which should be cut in two about the center of the bow). With your hand in this position you can squeeze the bow handle until you're blue in the face and you'll not torque it. But, as soon as you touch the handle with that area of the heel of your hand to the left of the center line, you begin to put side torquing pressure into it. If you shoot with your hand in this position, everything must be just exactly "so" or you'll have bad arrows and erratic shooting. The less hand contact you have on the grip, the better you'll shoot.

I personally set my bow into the "V" formed by the thumb and forefinger. I slide my hand somewhat to the left, around the handle a bit, so the pressure when the bow is drawn is basically on the base of the thumb. My hand is then tilted just slightly so the thumb is lower than my forefinger. I don't know that it's the best way to hold a bow...there must be a hundred ways to do it. So figure out what will work best for you, but remember this...the bow arm is the most important thing in shooting a bow...and the grip on the handle plays an important role in the stability of your bow arm.

Whether you use a tab or a glove is unimportant. I prefer a glove, but then I started with one, and the tab has never felt quite right to me. Use whichever works best for you. The positioning of the fingers onto the string is somewhat dictated by the position of the right arm and elbow. Ideally, the string should fit just at the forward edge of the first crease of the fingers. Unfortunately, the creases do not always line up just right, so you may end up

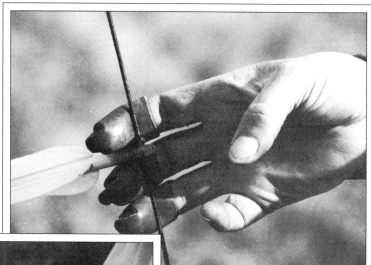

Normal "bite" on string with floating thumb.

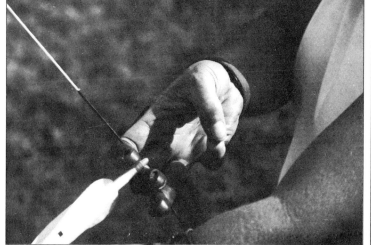

Thumb and little finger touching.

Deep hook on string with rigid thumb.

with one finger—probably the top one—riding on the pad forward of the creases. Some advise dropping the thumb down to ride on top of the little finger to give a more positive feel to the anchor. That doesn't work for me. As soon as my thumb goes down, my top finger turns into a claw that will not straighten. Keeping the drawing hand, the wrist and the fingers relaxed is important. Too much tension in those areas will result in your arrow coming off the rest as it is drawn...usually that happens at exactly the most inopportune moment. The only way I can avoid that tension is to allow my thumb to float when I'm drawing the bow. Getting a bigger bite/deeper hook on the string works for some shooters; certainly it is a stronger method of drawing. The problems with the deeper

hook are that it can be difficult to release properly and it also moves the string further from the face...which can cause you to shoot to the left. Shooting off the tips of the fingers is not recommended with heavier hunting weight bows because it is very difficult to relax the hand and the fingers during the drawing process. Avoid cocking your elbow too high as you draw. High elbows are bad habits. The drawing and shooting of a bow is best accomplished by a straight in-line motion. The bow arm and the drawing arm (along with the arrow) are in a straight line, pointing toward the target. It's a straight push and pull. A high right elbow defeats the whole principle of in-line drawing and shooting. With a high elbow, only half the body is pointed toward the target...the other half is

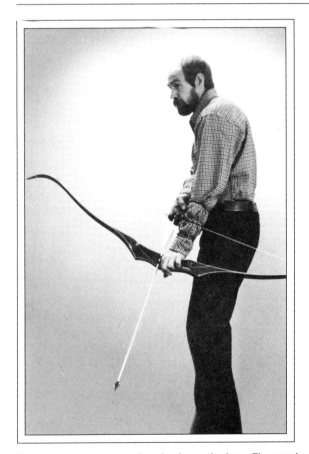

The author demonstrates how he draws the bow. The arm is down, elbow straight (almost locked) and the draw is begun with a ''stiff arm.''

waving at the sky. High right elbows also make it more difficult to isolate your back shooting muscles and it puts uneven pressure on your drawing fingers which often leads to a difficult release.

The left shoulder should be in its natural position. Do not allow it to slide in toward your chest or up toward the side of your face. Keeping your shoulder in the proper position is accomplished by pushing forward with the shoulder as the bow is drawn. The bow arm is the most important part of the bow shooting anatomy...the shoulder is one of the key parts of the bow arm. Sloppy shoulder positioning can result in arrows striking first one side of your target and then the other. In my personal shooting, I find that if my arrows begin wandering all over the target, normally all I have to do is begin thinking about pushing forward with my bow arm and the problem goes away.

Bringing the bow into play as the draw is begun can be accomplished in a number of ways. The "push-pull" method was the first taught. In the push-pull method, the bow is held with a bent left elbow, fairly close to the body. The fingers are on the string. The draw is begun by pushing forward (away from the body) with the bow arm and simultaneously drawing the string back toward the side of the face with the right arm. It is indeed a "push-pull" style. It is the method used by Fred Bear.

Another method is the "set-arm" style. In the set-arm method, the draw is begun with the bow already at arm's length in front of the shooter and pointing in the general direction of the target. With the bow already set in place, the archer draws the bow to anchor. My friend Bob Pitt shoots in this manner, and as I stated earlier, he's as good with a bow as most people ever get. My method is somewhere in between, my bow arm is fully extended, in an almost locked position...but it is down at my side. With my arm straight, I swing my bow arm straight up into position as I draw the bow to anchor. Howard Hill shot a bow in much this manner.

As to which method is best, ask a shooter copying Fred Bear, Bob Pitt or Howard Hill and you'll get three different answers. All three methods work. But all three probably will not work equally for you.

The bow is swung up towards the target and the draw is begun.

Give them all a try and select the one that feels best. I've tried them all and I think that the locked arm swing draw works best for my style of pure instinctive shooting. There are advantages and disadvantages to each.

Push-Pull Method: _Advantages_—Under stalking conditions the bow is held in a good position...in close to the body...ready to spring forward into action. If performed properly the motion required is minimal. **_Disadvantages_**—The position in which the bow is held in preparation for the draw tends to force the bow hand into a broken wrist position. Try as I might. I have not been able to hunt with my bow hand in the position I like using this method. This method also makes for sloppy shoulder placement, because the shoulder is not "set" before the draw is begun.

Set-Arm Method: *Advantages*—The set-arm method seems ideal for being very close to an animal and being able to get off a shot with minimal movement. The arm is in place and only the draw is required. Even with the method I use, I often find myself forced to shoot in this manner when I'm very near an animal. *Disadvantages*—This method can limit the amount of bow weight handled. It is, I think, a difficult method to use for purely instinctive shooting, since the bow and the arrow are actually "set" in the vicinity of the target prior to drawing and require that you switch your attention from the arrow to the target as you draw. My experience has been that by starting with the arrow within my vision I can't disregard it...and I begin using a form of "gap" or "point-of-aim" shooting. The set-arm method is not as conducive to shooting quickly or to shooting out of position.

Locked Arm-Swing Draw: *Advantages*—This emphasizes the in-line concept of instinctive shooting. Swinging with or at a moving target is very simple. Getting "on target" is particularly quick and simple. (The locked arm-swing method is the same style used by law enforcement people for quick combat shooting.) There's positive, consistent shoulder and bow arm position on each shot. It's perfect for tree stand shooting because the bow arm is, for the most part, already in the proper position. *Disadvantages*—When stalking in on an animal it is sometimes very difficult to keep the bow arm fully locked, extended and down at the side. The same factors can sometimes cause excessive motion in coming to full draw.

Anchor—The anchor is the rear sight on your bow. It is the tail end of the arrow, and as such, it has dramatic effects on the impact point of your arrow. Moving the anchor up or down creates down and up hits and moving it left to right causes right and left hits.

Set arm method

Looking over the arrow.

The draw.

Attention is shifted from the arrow to the target.

48

The anchor is the second factor in where your arrow will hit. The first factor is where you point your bow arm. All the other things you do when shooting a bow are really just furnishing assistance for the pointing procedure or to ensure consistent pointing of those two. That is not profound...but it is a factor that many people forget. I visualize the arrow as a telephone pole...you direct it by moving either the front end or the back end, or both. Don't make it more complicated than that.

The push-pull method of drawing. Note the bent elbow.

First off, I recommend anchoring with the middle finger in the corner of the mouth...or, at least, the middle finger as the major anchor indicator, in a place, in line with the corner of the mouth. Using the top or first finger in the corner of the mouth will work...and because of its lower position, does allow a smooth pull and release...but it is not the preferred or recommended method. Using your top finger puts the arrow too far from the eye and will give you problems with close shooting. With instinctive shooting, getting the eye and the arrow as close together as possible is important. Remember, the arrow is to be shot where the eye is looking. That ability is enhanced by having the eye and the arrow as close to the same plane as possible. That's why the middle finger in the corner of the mouth is better than the top finger. Trust me.

And maybe this is the place to talk about shooting three-fingers-under the nock. Three-fingers-under is exactly that...putting all three shooting fingers under the arrow, which moves the arrow even closer to the eye. Most people who use this method anchor very high...well up on the cheek bone, so they are looking down the arrow like a gun barrel. Following my line of reasoning about getting the arrow as near the eye as possible, wouldn't you have to say that three-fingers-under the nock would be better? It is a popular method and I know it is being used by a great many bowhunters. But, the original idea behind three-fingers-under was to get the arrow up near the eye and then sight down the length of the arrow at the target. "Gun barreling," it was called. While there is nothing wrong with that, it is a

departure from the instinctive style of shooting where the aiming is done automatically by the senses and no specific physical sighting device is used. I consider the end of the arrow a sight in this method. Therefore, for our purposes, I don't consider the method as instinctive shooting.

If the shooter is only using the three-fingers-under draw as an anchor closer to the eye, and is not looking down the arrow, then I guess you have to say it's just another possible instinctive anchor. But, for some reason, the anchor just doesn't work as well or as smoothly as it should. Perhaps it's because the three-fingers-under the nock anchor is a bit too high, making it difficult to release sharply...or maybe it's because all three fingers are on the same plane...I don't know. Perhaps, a more important consideration is that good arrow flight is often difficult to attain and that the method is particularly

loud shooting. However, many bowhunters will still use it...and that's fine...and tell me that I'm full of beans and that three-fingers-under is the only way to shoot. Go for it.

Many shooters, besides using their middle finger in the corner of the mouth anchor, find that having another spot on their face as a secondary indicator of the same solid anchor is a good idea. You may find that placing your depressed thumb behind the angle of the jawbone, as well as placing your finger in the corner of the mouth, gives a good secure anchor. The thumb is allowed to come in under the jawbone and rest, sort of, against the neck. The length of your hand and the depth of your hook onto the string can be a factor. If I take a very deep

hook onto the string, I cannot get my thumb behind my jawbone and still have my fingers in the corner of my mouth.

A good idea is to find yourself a very lightweight bow and play around with getting a positive anchor. The lightweight bow will allow you to "search around" on your face and at the corner of your mouth, for a good, solid, repeatable anchor. Doing the same thing with your hunting bow is not as easy. Find an anchor spot you can get to as you come straight back with your draw. Avoid any anchor that is accomplished by overdrawing the bow slightly and then sinking forward back along the face into a place. That was a common error among field archers in the '60s. It can be done with lightweight

Push-pull method. The bow is pushed forward with one hand as the draw is begun with the other. The bow is pushed at the target and the draw occurs as a simultaneous movement.

The ''three fingers under'' the nock.

Top finger anchor.

Using the middle finger as anchor.

bows, but even then not very well. Avoid it...you're losing back tension when you slide forward to your anchor point...and that is not good.

Aiming: I guess we have to use the word "aiming." Personally, I think of the word in terms of the use of some sort of mechanical or physical system. And instinctive aiming certainly isn't that. Instinctive aiming is accomplished by feel...feel based on physical and mental memory. It's a product of having done this same thing before.

You aim instinctively by concentrating, with both eyes open, on your target and allowing your bow arm to automatically make the trajectory adjustments necessary. Because your arm and your arrow are a single unit (your arrow is down almost on top of your hand), you are simply pointing your arm...and the arrow goes where your arm is pointed. One of the most important aspects of shooting instinctively is concentrating your aim/ your eye on the smallest spot you can see in the center of your target. The more intense your concentration on a specific small part of your target and the more you are able to block out the rest of your target, the better you will find yourself shooting.

Years ago, when I was just learning to shoot the bow and arrow, a number of us had gathered, just prior to deer season, for a little practice. I was a complete beginner and had no intention of hunting deer that year. I'd planned to practice my shooting and see what I could find out about deer and then give it a try the following year. Looking back, I suspect others in the group would have been well advised to do the same. We were shooting all our arrows at a plastic wastebasket stuffed with papers. On occasion, a stray arrow would strike the target...mostly, we were holding a four-foot group at 15 yards. Then my brother threw an empty red cigarette pack on the ground near the wastebasket and I let one fly at it. I almost fell over when I hit it. As the practice session continued, I found that I could consistently hit or shoot very close to the small cigarette package, but I still couldn't hit the plastic wastebasket with any degree of regularity. It was a long time later before I figured out that the smaller cigarette package had focused my concentration on a single spot. The much larger wastebasket didn't do that. Now I know the secret was that I didn't pick an exact spot on the wastebasket and concentrate totally on that spot as I shot.

Intense, quivering concentration on the **very center** of your target is absolutely necessary to achieve any sort of instinctive shooting skill. Every fiber of your body needs to be tuned to that tiny place. You can't get by with shooting at a place behind a deer's foreleg...you must concentrate on and shoot for a single hair in that location.

One of the things I do to bring my concentration homing in on a spot is to flex my knees or squat somewhat as I draw and shoot. It can really help you align yourself with the arrow and your target, but perhaps more importantly, it intensifies concentration and simplifies directing it at a specific spot. Try this. Stand bolt upright and point your finger at a spot on the wall. As you can see, you can do a fair job of aligning your extended finger with the spot on the wall. Now flex your knees, tilt your head forward and point at the same spot. Quite a difference, eh? With the knees bent and the head slightly forward, everything is directed exactly in a straight line. Like the locked-arm swing draw, flexing the knees to intensify the concentration is part of the "combat stance" taught by police departments. Utilize hand-eye coordination by getting everything in a straight line. Pointing exactly where you're looking is what it is.

To effect the degree of concentration necessary for shot after shot accuracy requires practice. The mechanics of shooting the bow...that is, the draw, the anchor and release...must be automatic. Once you've passed the learning stage, thinking about how you are going to draw the bow, where your anchor should be and how long to aim doesn't allow space in your brain for concentration on your target. As soon as your shooting style becomes implanted and automatic, your accuracy will improve considerably. When I haven't shot for a while, I find that I have to spend a while just working on the shooting mechanics. As soon as I begin shooting without thinking through each step, then I can start

Bending your knees, as in Picture 2, as you draw helps hone your concentration on a spot. It helps you align yourself with your arrow and target. Picture 1 shows unbent knees.

worrying about accuracy. What I'm trying to point out is that the kind of concentration required for instinctive shooting must be total. There is no room for mentally running through the shooting procedure on each shot.

Many bowhunters say they see their arrow when they shoot. Others say they are aware of the arrow's presence in their secondary vision. That is, their concentration is on the target, but they see a more or less blurred arrow shaft and they are aware of its presence. Most say they use it "sort of" for alignment. My friend Bob Pitt shoots this way.

It seems that many of the shooters who are aware of their arrow in their secondary vision are using the set-arm method of drawing the bow, so maybe we should take a minute to talk about that method, which is somewhat different from pure instinctive shooting. Haugen and Metcalf, in their book **Field Archery and Bowhunting**, talk about what I am calling the set-arm method and relate it to the pre-draw gap system of shooting. I believe that most shooters who use the set-arm method of drawing are basically using the pre-draw gap system of instinctive shooting (See page 48.) In the pre-draw gap system, shooters set the bow-arm out straight with their fingers on the string, and, more or less, look out over the arrow toward the target. The bow

53

and the arrow are pointed in general relationship to the target. The shooter, always keeping both eyes open, uses the arrow as a reference for alignment and elevation before the bow is drawn. This sighting is done over and across the point of the arrow... never down the full length. As the bow is drawn, the attention is directed away from the arrow and the bow and is brought to bear totally on the target. Before the arrow is released, the shooter's total concentration is on his target and he allows his instinctive eye to make the final adjustments before shooting.

So the pre-draw gap method of instinctive shooting begins with the use of the arrow as a reference, but then switches to an instinctive adjustment for fine tuning before the shot. Which is why I said it is somewhat of a variation of instinctive shooting. (There is also a post-draw gap system of shooting in which the arrow is used after the draw much like a sight would be used. This method has nothing whatsoever to do with instinctive shooting and is used/was used mainly in competitive archery.)

Personally, I shoot by concentrating totally on my target, never seeing the arrow at all. I concentrate on what I want to hit. Without breaking my concentration, I swing my arm up toward the target and at the same time I am drawing the bow toward my anchor and flexing my knees simultaneously. By the time my hand has reached my anchor, my bow arm is already on target. I barely touch my anchor before the arrow is gone. Others hold for just a moment to aim. Speed isn't really what we're seeking, although sometimes it is helpful to be able to shoot quickly. I shoot quicker than most because I've shot about a billion arrows in this manner and because I'm aiming as I draw (which is what I'm going to teach you to do). When I get to my anchor, it's time! Interestingly enough, I don't feel as though I shoot quickly. Others say I do. I have developed a style and a rhythm over the years that appears to be almost snap shooting, but is actually a controlled instinctive shot, executed in a single motion.

Release: The release is effected by turning loose of the string...allowing it to suddenly leave the fingers. It probably happens best when the fingers are simply relaxed, allowing the weight of the bow to pull the string from the fingers. At this stage it becomes increasingly important that you are using an in-line draw. If your right arm and elbow are basically in line with your left (bow arm), the release will be smooth and crisp. A right elbow which is too high will create problems here. If you've shot more than once or twice before this, you probably have a feel for the release. Sometimes it seems like an impossible thing for the beginner, but in a few shots they find that it just sort of begins to happen. They think..."Well, I think I'll relea..." and it's already gone.

We spend far too much time worrying about the release. It is the subject of pages and pages of study and commentary. And, yes...a bad release is a real problem for many people. But everyone seems to be looking at the wrong way of correcting the problem. Think about this...

For every action there is an equal and opposite reaction.

Read that about a dozen times and try to place it properly into what you're doing with a bow and arrow when you shoot. Allow me. The bow arm is pushed forward and the string is pulled back...two opposite actions. As long as you continue to push forward with the bow arm, the release hand will easily turn loose of the string. It is not possible to do otherwise. (And let me add here that the term "hold" is a misnomer...you do not "hold" in archery. Holding is static...shooting a bow is dynamic. It is a push-pull action and it must remain so, from beginning to end. You do not "hold" the bow at full draw and then release. **Your bow hand must be pushing forward and your release hand must be pulling back.**)

If, let us say, you jerk your bow arm to the left, I guarantee you that your release will jump to the right (opposite reaction). You cannot jerk your bow arm to one side and still have a straight back, crisp release. **Nor can you jerk your release to one side if your bow arm is pushing forward.** You may want to read through that again. Simplified, what I have said is that as long as you push forward with your bow arm, your release will take care of

In-line draw. Note the straight line between the arrow, bow arm, anchor and head.

itself. If your release seems to be turning sour, look to your bow arm. As soon as you get it under control, the release will be fine.

Let's start bringing what you've learned about form and technique together now.

As mentioned, it's best if you can get your hands on a very lightweight bow for the early stages of learning instinctive shooting. We want to concentrate totally on form, on doing the same thing over and over again. That is more easily accomplished with less drawing weight. You will shoot at a small target, but at only 10 to 20 feet...and we aren't really concerned about whether or not you hit it. This is for form only.

You'll need:

*Your bow (a light one if possible)

*Glove/tab and armguard

***One** arrow

*A practice butt...preferably three bales high, or if you have one of the smaller portable targets, get it up onto something, so it's at eye level. Cover over any target that may already be imprinted there. Your target should be one spot...perhaps a crumpled cigarette pack, or just make a small solid dot with a felt tip marker. Make it no larger than your thumb nail—smaller might be better. Assume your shooting stance, bow in hand, at a distance no greater than 20 feet in front of the practice butt. Begin without an arrow on the string. We want to go through the proper form a few times without the worry of shooting an arrow or hitting the target. But you should still concentrate on the small spot. We'll use the locked-arm swing draw method. Here's what I want you to do:

1. Your bow arm is rigid, in place, down near your side, ready to begin.

2. Your drawing hand is on the string at the proper place. (No arrow just yet.)

3. As you begin to draw the bow, you also begin to swing the bow up and toward the target.

4. The bow comes up slightly quicker, so that when it is "on target," the drawing hand must finish the draw by coming straight back to the anchor. In other words, when the bow is basically straight out in front of you, the drawing hand should be just passing your nose (or thereabouts) and the draw is completed with a straight pull to the anchor. All of this is done in one smooth motion. You do not pull the string three-fourths of the way and stop, waiting for the bow arm to get on target. One smooth swing up with the bow, as the string is drawn to anchor. Because of draw length, the timing of your draw and anchor might be slightly different than what I've described. Play with it a bit and you'll find what feels smooth to you.

5. Go through that swing draw and anchor a few times until you have the feel for the timing of it. And then begin adding bending your knees as you draw. You'll immediately notice how much better you are now aligned with the arrow your target as you draw.

6. Now...put the arrow on the string and add canting the bow and head position to the draw and anchor. Cant the upper limb of the bow to about two o'clock (just exactly how much the bow should be canted is a personal thing and will vary from person to person). With the bow canted, just before you reach your anchor, lean your head slightly forward and down to bring your eye directly over the arrow and your anchor. With your bow canted you are now looking exactly over the arrow and at your target. Rather than thinking, "He said to cant the bow this much and lean the head that much"

...think in terms of canting the bow and leaning into and over the arrow to the place where you feel an obvious exact alignment with your body and your arrow...a straight shot to your target. It is not stiff and precise ... it is casual and easy. You are wrapping yourself and your bow and your arrow all together...you become a single, natural coordinated unit.

7. You may begin concentrating on your target and shooting whenever you feel ready. Stay very close to the target and think about the mechanics. Feel the movement, direct everything in-line toward that spot.

Rhythm and timing are very important in instinctive shooting. The speed at which you draw the bow will affect everything that happens thereafter. Let me explain: It throws everything out of kilter if you jerk the bow back, hard and fast, and then try to aim slowly (yes, I know...you see people do that). Try it...it fouls up the complete feel of shooting, doesn't it? Work at developing a rhythm to your shooting. From draw, through anchor, to release, the speed of your movement should be constant. The faster you draw...the faster you should shoot. A slow, steady draw should be finalized with a slower anchor and release. Work at that...it's important. Actually, the rhythm usually comes naturally...you have to work at making it jerky and out-of-sync. So, relax...let it happen.

Utilizing your back muscles, as opposed to your arms when you shoot, is something you should work hard at developing. If you've been shooting for a while you already know that.

> However, it may be more important when shooting instinctively than with other shooting to just "let things happen"...the need to focus all your attention on your target and to allow the mechanics of drawing and anchoring to work automatically.

I think the let-off characteristics of the compound bow have gotten many bowhunters away from thinking about using their back muscles when they shoot. The draw should be basically performed by use of the deltoid and the trapezius (shoulder and back) muscles, with minimal help from the arm. The arm and the hand should be little more than linkage between the bow string and those muscles. Make yourself exaggerate the relaxing of the drawing arm and the hand...to the point where they cannot pull the bow. Then the back muscles are forced into the act. And again...as we talked about in the release section...for every action there is an equal and opposite reaction. If you **push** with the bow arm side of your body, you will **pull** with the opposite side. Just be sure that the pulling is done with the back and not with the arm.

I place a lot of emphasis on the in-line aspect of my shooting. The bow arm, the head and the drawing arm should be kept as nearly straight "in-line" during shooting as possible. Everything, in-line, pointing collectively on the same plane, at the same

object. Practice your draw and anchor in front of a mirror, without your bow. Note the location of your shoulders. Are they "in-line"? One way to look at this in-line concept is to stand straight with your head up and extend your bow arm straight out. Next, place your drawing arm in an exact straight line with your release hand in line with, but slightly in front of, your right shoulder. Now bend your knees and move your head to your drawing hand. That's an exaggerated move to show you what "in-line" means.

Well, you've got the basics now. I know there are a lot of words and a lot of "do's and don't's" in this chapter, so continue to read and re-read it as you practice instinctive shooting. I'd recommend that you stay very close to your target for awhile, at least until you feel the technique is ingrained. Don't be afraid to return to close shooting anytime you feel things aren't working just right. And remember I don't know a single instinctive shooter who has problems because he shoots/practices too much.

7

The author and his 1971 Indiana whitetail.

Setting Up And Tuning Your Bow

Recurve bows are such simple things. They're not much more than a piece of wood with a swerve at each end and a string tying the ends together that allows it to shoot an arrow straight forward when it's drawn and released smoothly. A recurve bow is just about as simple as you can get when it comes to shooting an arrow. In today's world of technological complexity, recurve bows are a refreshing escape backward into yesterday's simpler technology...a reminder of a time when the quality of a man's labor was directly related to the sum of his reward. Simple, straight-forward and honest, with no wheels, cams, wires or what-have-you to get between you and getting the arrow into the place you want it to be. A recurve bow is about as simple to keep running properly as an old V8 Ford...but better, because you don't have to grease or oil it or put gas in it. They're a nice little bit of simplistic, uncomplicated, direct labor, with a little bit of dignified beauty thrown in.

Things don't get a lot simpler than the recurve, we've established that. Great! Just pull it back to your ear and turn it loose. That's all you do...right?

Well, not exactly. It's **practically** that simple ...almost. Certainly by comparison to much of today's modern equipment, the recurve is utter simplicity. But you don't just pull it out of the box, put a string on it and instantly begin to hit everything you shoot at. It is slightly more complex.

But **just** slightly. There are a few things, a few adjustments, that are necessary.

Recurve bows can be tinkered with...and they should be. They can be made to shoot better...or worse, if you choose. They are adjustable...not on a grand scale like a compound bow, but noticeably. The difference between a properly tuned and an untuned recurve can be huge...and yet some would say it's a subtle thing that requires close attention to arrow flight and to feel and sound. But then, you see, recurves that are "out of tune" don't do wild, crazy things. A recurve out of tune isn't some sort of unmanageable thing that will require a Mr. Goodwrench and leaving it overnight. It's not hard to tune a recurve. It's fairly straightforward. There are only a few things you can adjust on a recurve, but what you can do will greatly affect your ability to shoot the bow accurately and perhaps more importantly it can increase your enjoyment.

Nocking point and brace height (fistmele) are the two major factors that will affect your bow's performance. The brace height and the nocking point sort of work together. As the brace height is adjusted by lengthening and shortening the string, the nock point moves up and down slightly. Not much, but a little. If the brace height is too low, arrow flight is erratic and can confound your attempt to find the proper nock point. As you learn about tuning recurves and begin to get the feel for it, you'll find that you sort of do the two—nock point and brace height— simultaneously.

But, we can't start out that way. It has to be one step at a time. So let's start with the nock point.

Nock Points

The nock point's location is basic to shooting any bow; it's the first and foremost requirement. When I set up a new bow, the nock point's location is my starting point after I do a little preliminary brace-height adjustment. Measure the brace height on your bow and make sure it is within the range recommended by the manufacturer. If it is too low (if they recommend seven to eight inches and it is now six and one-half inches) twist the string to shorten it. Don't worry for now if it is a little bit too high. We'll come back to the brace height later.

Finding the proper location for your nocking point is a simple matter. The nocking point locates the nock end of your arrow on the string in the same place for each shot. It does nothing else. But you'll never shoot well without having it in the proper place. It was quite a common thing in the early days of bowhunting to run into guys who'd been shooting a bow for years and had never used, or heard of, a nock point. I remember a hunting trip to Alaska with a fellow who was president of a large archery company who never used a nock point. "Aaaw, that's all a bunch of crap," he'd say. "If you point the SOB in the right direction, it'll go there." Simple logic. But without a nock point you can't point the thing "in the right direction" twice in a row. If you put your nock point too high or too low, your arrows will flip up and down in flight (it's called "porpoising). Generally, that up and down motion is the only direct effect you'll ever see from an incorrect setting. Of course, that up and down arrow flight will cause all kinds of shooting problems, including arrows that strike the target in a tilted up or down attitude and arrows with broadheads that do crazy things.

Start by forgetting all preconceived notions about how high or low your nock point should be. The idea that everyone should be able to shoot their bows with their nock point one-eighth of an inch

above 90 degrees was, no doubt, started by someone selling something.

Your nock point should be located at the point from which your arrow shoots best. Period.

You need an archer's T-square to do this properly, so if you don't have one, I'd suggest you invest in one immediately. I am only familiar with the Potawatomi Bow Square, but I'm sure there are others which will work fine. They're indispensable for installing and checking nocking points and brace height. The T-square is similar to a doctor's stethoscope...you listen to the bow's heartbeat with it. When the bow sounds wrong, you use the T-square to check the brace height. If the arrow jumps around in flight, your T-square will tell you if your nock point has slipped on you. It's a rare day when I'm shooting and don't have a T-square within reaching distance. Get one and keep it handy.

Okay, let's look at nock point.

I recommend that you locate your nock point above your arrow...that you nock under the nock point. Putting your nock point below the arrow doesn't work well under hunting conditions. With a heavy broadhead sitting out there on the end of your arrow, the nock—and the arrow—will slide up the string, out of place, everytime you aren't holding it. Some like the security of two nock points...one

A nock point will help you shoot consistently, but where that nock point is located is an individual decision.

above and one below. They work fine as long as you always have time to look down and watch where you locate your arrow. If, in a hurry, you nock your arrow below the wrong locator, you're in a heap of trouble. That mistake ought to put your arrow just about six inches to a foot right over the top of his back at 12 yards.

Start by putting a temporary nock locator—a pencil mark or a piece of tape will do—at about three-eighths of an inch above 90 degrees. Don't try guessing. Use a T-square. A target butt or a dirt bank of about shoulder height is the ideal place to check arrow flight. Stand about 15 yards from the target. Standing closer doesn't seem to work as well, because your eye needs time to see the arrow in flight before it strikes the target. Bright, visible fletching will help. I find that fletching of all one color is better, also. An odd-colored cock feather sometimes gives the illusion of an unstable arrow. Shoot a few arrows with a three-eighths of an inch nock point and see what happens. It is a good idea to have a second person watch your arrow while you actually shoot at a target. There is a tendency for some shooters, if they're trying to watch their arrows in flight, to jerk their bow hand down and their head up as they shoot, causing bad arrow flight with the best of set-ups. I think it is good to actually shoot at a target. That will give you a better feel for where your arrow is going in relation to where you are aiming. If your nock point is correct for you, your arrows will fly straight and true. If it's not, they'll seem to be hopping up and down for the first 10 or so feet before they straighten up. Shoot several arrows. If even a single arrow has a little bounce to it, you'd best move the nock point up a little higher. Move the temporary nock point up to one-half inch and give that a try. If your arrows fly well at half an inch you might just stay there. I think I'd move the thing up another little bit, however, just to see if it gets better or worse. Adjust the nock point up and down until your arrows are flying true. Don't be afraid to put your nock point at whatever place your arrows shoot best. There is no exactly right or exactly wrong place. Because each of us shoots a little differently, we may each find a slightly different "best" location for our nock point. For example, if you shoot with a particularly high elbow

(which will cause an abnormal amount of downward pressure on the nock by the top finger) you may well be putting a slight bend in your arrow at full draw...which will cause the arrow to sort of rebound off the arrow rest upon release, requiring a higher than normal nock point. If you set the heel of your hand down into the bow more than I do, you'll probably have to shoot a higher nock point than I will, because your hand pressure is changing the way the limbs of the bow recover.

A variety of things can come into play on just why you shoot well with a three-eighths of an inch above 90 degrees nock point and I need mine set at half an inch. I used to shoot with a fellow who shot with his nock point such that his arrow was at exactly 90 degrees and he shot very well. That is unusual. In fact, I've not seen another person do it (if he was shooting off the shelf). Once you become consistent in your shooting style, you'll probably find that your nock point will be the same from bow to bow, year in and year out. I have personally set my nock point at one-half inch above 90 degrees for at least the last 20 years.

Your shaft size and nock size have a direct effect on where you place your nock point. Consider that hunting arrows vary from 5/16 to 23/64 of an inch in diameter. Let us say, for example, that you and I are both trying to shoot our bows with a nock point three-eighths of an inch above 90 degrees. You are shooting a 2018 (which is 5/16 of an inch in diameter) and I am shooting a 2317 (which is 23/64 of an inch in diameter). When you put your arrow on the string, below the nock point, the bottom of your arrow—which is 5/16 high—is one-sixteenth of an inch above 90 degrees. This will work for some people. On the other hand, my arrow, the 2317, (which is 23/64 high in diameter) is one sixty-fourth of an inch **below** 90 degrees. This will not work at all. Keep an eye on shaft size. If you change arrows and bad things begin happening, you know where to begin looking.

There are commercially made nock points on the market. The heat-shrink type always worked well for me, but they are hard to find these days. The type that squeeze onto the string are the most popular. I think they all require a tool to put them into place. As near as I've seen, they all work well. These days I've taken to making my own nock point with dental floss or a fine thread. I work glue into the wraps of thread as I go and find that they are very solid. Whatever you use, make sure it is located firmly so it won't move. If you occasionally have problems with the string center serving slipping on you—which will cause your nock point's locations to move—work a little glue into the warps on the center serving with your fingers. Your problems should disappear.

However...don't put a permanent nock point on just yet. Let's wait until we get the brace height figured out. Then you can stick on your nock point.

Brace Height

Brace height is the most important possible variable in a recurve bow. Brace height, or fistmele, is the distance in inches from the string to the bow when the bow is strung. The Archery Manufacturers Organization (AMO) specifies that the brace height measurement be taken from the string to the center of the plunger-button hole...which leaves out a lot of traditional equipment. Some recurve manufacturers measure it from the deepest part of the grip to the string. In our shop, we measure it from the string to the back of the sight window. One manufacturer even measures it from the butt of the handle to the string. You need to know where the manufacturer of your bow measures from, but basically it is only important that **you** measure from the same place all the time.

Brace height can be adjusted by using a longer or shorter string or by twisting and untwisting the string (which shortens and lengthens the string). The brace height of your bow will affect the following:

(1) Arrow flight

(2) Arrow speed

(3) Bow noise

(4) Stability and feel of the bow

(5) Life and longevity of the bow

How can brace height affect all of these things? Well, to begin with, visualize two different bows...one with a brace height of 12 inches and one with a brace height of six inches. When an arrow

is shot from the bow with the 12-inch brace height, the string actually stops going forward (pushing the arrow) 12 inches (the brace height) from the back of the bow. Think of the distance from your anchor point (from which the arrow was released) to that 12-inch brace height as the bow's "power stroke." Along with the bending of the limb, that power stroke is what is propelling your arrow. A 28-inch draw with a 12-inch brace height has a 16-inch stroke.

Now, visualize shooting the bow with the six-inch brace height. The string, upon release, travels from the 28-inch draw to the six-inch brace height...a "power stroke" of 22 inches. Quite a difference!

Compare the two. You could say that the bow with the 12-inch brace height is, by comparison, flipping the arrow. It's similar to snapping or flipping your wrist. The bow with the six-inch brace height is using a much longer stroke that continues to push the arrow longer and for a greater distance. You could say the arrow is being "powered" for a longer period of time. The two bows were basically built alike...but brace height has made them very different bows.

Now, normally you'll not be looking at a six-inch difference between where you're now shooting your bow and where it ought to be. I use the bows with the six-inch brace height and the 12-inch brace

A too high elbow will cause an abnormal amount of downward pressure on the nock by the top finger.

height for illustration purposes only. Although most recurve shooters I encounter are shooting their bows too high...normally. If they'd drop them down an inch or a half-inch, they'd often find the bow shooting better. Brace height, in most recurves, can do more to affect the performance of the bow than all other adjustments combined.

Simply stated, you can say that the brace height of your bow determines how long the string "stays with" or keeps pushing your arrow. The lower your brace height, the longer the string stays with your arrow. I think this is desirable with heavy hunting arrows. The longer the string continues to push the heavier hunting arrow, the better performance/ speed you'll achieve. The higher brace height probably works well with lightweight target equipment. Let me give you an example: If you toss a small, lightweight rock by simply snapping your wrist, you'll sometimes be able to throw it farther than by using a long, complete overhead arm motion. If you try using a heavier rock with the wrist snap, the results change completely. The rock goes no place. Long, powerful movements work best for heavier things, arrows included. Short, snappy movements will move lighter objects better. I think you can use those same principles to understand why bows with lower brace heights shoot faster.

So...if that's true, why not just put a long string on every bow and shoot them with a three and one-half inch brace height? It doesn't work that way. When I talk about low brace height, I mean the lowest brace height at which a given bow will perform properly.

Just **exactly** where the lowest brace height **is** varies from bow to bow and from manufacturer to manufacturer. No two bows are ever exactly the same. The right brace height for a given bow is largely a product of how the bow was originally designed and built. All kinds of other things, including your shooting style and the number of accessories you have attached to your bow, will also have a bearing on what works best for you. However, no matter what type of recurve bow it is, the brace height can be adjusted up and down and it will affect the bow's performance.

There will be a specific brace height at which

you'll feel your bow performs best. You'll have to play around with it a bit. Supposedly, the manufacturer's recommendations on brace height should be in the ballpark. I hate to say it, but that isn't always true. One major manufacturer provides a string that braces their bow at 10-1/2 to 11 inches. But putting a string on the bow that lowers it to eight and one-half inches improves both the feel and the performance by at least 50 percent.

And I guess this is as good a place as any to talk about strings and string lengths. What do you do if the string that comes with your bow is too short (e.g., with no twists in the string the bow is still braced at 17 inches)? The bow I just mentioned came with a string that braced it at 10-1/2 to 11 inches. I guess you could call that manufacturer and see if you can get another string. But I suspect you'd be ahead of the game if you go to an archery shop and try to find something that fits your bow. Take your bow with you. Most of the shops you'll go into have their recurve strings (if they have any at all) by actual length of the string, not by the bow length ...which makes about as much sense as putting auto parts under the size of the car's gas cap rather than their model, etc. It's a really dumb system and a pet peeve of mine. We'd best not get into it here. Anyway...find a string that's too long, so you can wind it up. Later, you can have someone make strings that are specifically for your bow.

The string is shortened by taking it off the bow and twisting it. This will shorten the string. The first few twists will have little effect, but as you begin to take up the slack in the string, each twist will raise your brace height a bit. Twist it a little and then put it back on the bow. Pull it a few times and then measure the brace height. Still too low? Take the string off and do it again, and so forth, until you have it where you want it. You lengthen the string in just the opposite manner...by untwisting it. Be cautious if your bow has a flemish splice string on it. The twisting is what holds the string together. Normally, when you receive a string it will be at its longest. There will be a small amount of stretch, but that's probably all. Experiment a little. Take it very, very low and see what happens...and then take it really high. That's how you'll learn about your bow. Now...keep in mind that with some bows the brace height that will feel best to you and be the quietest is in only one spot; i.e., seven inches feels too low, but seven and one-eighth inches may be just right...even though seven and one-quarter doesn't seem any better than seven inches did. So go up and down in small increments.

If you brace the bow **too** low, you'll get bad arrow flight, excessive noise and vibration. When the bow is braced very low, you'll notice that the limbs seem to continue vibrating after the arrow has been shot. The bad arrow flight is usually obvious. You'll hear the arrow smacking the side of the bow and notice the arrow tail-wagging too much in flight. The string is staying with the arrow too long. Take a couple of twists in the string and generally your arrows will straighten right up. The excessive noise is caused by the amount of string that is laying in the recurved portion of the limb and by the amount of shock created by the extra string contact. The vibration is caused by the same thing and by the fact that the low brace height is allowing the tips of the limbs to come too far forward of their natural designed position. Again, you should twist/raise the brace height a bit.

Personally, I start by bracing my bow as low as I can. Low enough so I **am** getting bad arrow flight and noise. **Then** I twist the string up until everything clears up. For me, that is often where I get the best feel and performance from my bow.

The lower brace height will make your bow pull easier. Some of the difference is actually poundage. (We've found at Bighorn that when weighing a new bow we can get about a pound difference by changing the brace height about an inch.) Mostly the bow just feels better. If your bow feels a little stout and uncomfortable, drop the brace height as much as you can...it'll feel better. Some bowhunters do, however, prefer the feel of their bow at a higher brace height. Just as some bowhunters like their bows braced so low that the limbs dance and vibrate for five seconds after they shoot. It's an individual sport...always has been, always will be.

You will also probably get more speed from your bow at the lower brace height. Again, this is, I believe, caused by the string staying behind the

arrow, pushing it longer. However, if you go **too** low you'll lose speed. This is because the string, when braced too low, begins interfering with the paradox and the flight of the arrow and thus the arrow loses stability and then speed.

Generally speaking, a lower brace height will make your bow shoot faster and pull easier. A higher brace height will usually make your bow quieter and will eliminate arrow flight problems if you go high enough (assuming properly matched arrows). The higher brace height makes a quieter bow because...

1. The string is touching less of the limb. When the bow is braced higher, the limb is bent more and the string is shorter.

2. The limb itself is not flexing as much. The distance from strung position to full draw and then back to resting strung position is shorter with the higher brace height.

3. The string and the limb remain in a more compressed—or taut—position and this allows less vibration and movement.

Arrow flight problems are fewer with the higher brace height because...

1. The length of time the string is in contact with the arrow is reduced.

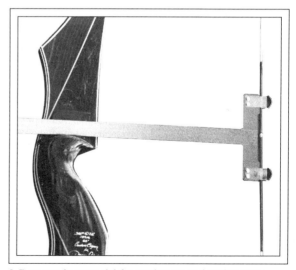

A T-square is essential for setting up and tuning your recurve.

2. That short "flip" and then release, by the string, creates a "free flying" arrow, which has more time to correct itself (if you released badly) and one which is more capable of comforming to the rest and going into the paradox properly.

If you don't want to mess around with all the adjusting and experimenting, you should just twist the string up as high as you can. For some that is preferable. But you should expect it to pull harder and probably shoot slower.

If your bow is center shot and you are shooting arrows properly matched to your bow, you'll have little need for any kind of adjustment for your arrow plate on the inside of your sight window. Remember, we're talking about hunting arrows out of hunting weight bows. It's become a popular theory these days that a bow should be cut well past center. An amount of this is okay...I guess. But unless you are trying to shoot arrows that are underspined for your bow, there is no need to be much more than center shot. I see no reason that a bowhunter shooting a hunting bow needs anything more elaborate than a center shot bow. Cutting a bow past center and then selling you some device to move the arrow back to center has always been suspect to me. Hmmm.

Having a bow center shot, or nearly so, is a good thing. A bow that is not center shot will be more critical of arrow spine. That is, you'll have to be more exacting in your selection of the proper arrow. That is because as the amount of center shot in a bow decreases, the amount of paradox the arrow will go through is increased...and as the amount of paradox increases, the more important it becomes that your arrows be exactly identical so they will all perform the same. Longbows, because they are not center shot, are much more critical on arrow matching than are center shot recurves. That isn't the end of the world. Once you've matched the arrow to the bow, it can still be shot well. But the bow's lack of center shot characteristics cost you a little. You see, while cutting the sight window in close to center widens the arrow selection possibilities, it also puts the arrow closer to the center of the bow and more directly behind the

force of the bowstring. And there is some obvious advantage to that. Anyway...

It should be mentioned here that there are bow manufacturers who claim that a bow shouldn't be completely center shot and that they achieve their best performance when the arrow is forced to go through an amount of paradox. The testing of Hickman, Nagler and Klopsteg, as reported in their book, **Archery, the Technical Side** does not support that position. Nor does my own personal shooting experience. I find that as long as a bow is fairly close to being center shot, I have no problems with it. But when I get over an arrow width away from being center shot, things begin happening that I don't like.

If you are shooting an elevated rest of some type and your bow is properly center shot, you should have no problems getting decent arrow flight. If you are shooting off the shelf you will have to also set up the arrow plate that goes on the inside of the sight window above the shelf. I use a thin leather or moleskin arrow plate. I put a tiny (paper match size or smaller) piece of leather under the plate...so as to create a slightly raised point **straight above the deepest part of the grip**. Putting a pressure point in that particular place goes a long way toward minimizing problems caused by torquing the bow in your hand.

Let me explain. If you torque the bow in your hand as you shoot, the least amount of bow movement is at the pivot created by the bow hand and the bow handle. Any point farther in front of that point, or farther behind that point, will move a great deal more. It also creates a single point of contact on the side of the bow...as opposed to riding against the arrow plate all the way across the bow.

Matching your arrow to your bow is very important. An often quoted comment is that the arrow is more important than the bow. I agree with that. While it is very important and will affect the final performance of your bow, coming up with the proper arrow shouldn't be a problem. For the most part, it should be as simple as asking your local archery dealer for a little assistance. He has all the information necessary to give you the proper arrow for your particular bow. There are aluminum and wood arrows to match any weight bow and any draw length. If you want to shoot wood arrows, my experience has been that you'll probably need to contact someone who specializes in them. I would go a step further and repeat something I said in another chapter. If you are in the process of changing bows, particularly if you are going from a compound to a recurve, I would recommend that you stay with the arrows you've been shooting, if at all possible. Don't throw too many variables into the pot at the same time. A new bow **and** different arrows can make it hard to put your finger on just where a specific problem lies. Once you get that new bow tuned and shooting just right, **then** take a look at adding another variable (the arrows).

Most serious bowhunters recommend a heavy arrow for hunting, as opposed to a lighter one. That's pretty well in line with what we've been told for the last 30 years. Heavy arrows penetrate better. That is true. However...there is a very good argument which says that lighter arrows shoot faster and flatter and thus reduce the shooting margin of error...by a much greater percentage than adding weight to an arrow increases penetration. It gets pretty technical...too much so for my tastes. I stay pretty close to the old rule of thumb...10 grains for each pound of bow weight on bows up to about 60 pounds and about nine grains, or thereabouts, on heavier bows. I like an arrow of around 600 grains. I normally shoot draw weights between 65 and 70-some pounds.

I tend to shy away from arrows that are marginally spined for my bow. If an arrow seems a little close on spine, I'll jump to the next larger size. When I shot aluminum, I could shoot a 2117 with a field point. But, with broadheads and a poor release, they'd sometimes jump to the left a little. It just never seemed wise to me to even consider shooting 2117s...so I used the 2219. And don't worry if you need to shoot a heavier spined arrow, or a weaker spined arrow, than your buddy, who shoots the same exact weight. That is not unusual. Variances in shooting styles, release, draw length, etc. all play a part. Ron Montross, a good friend from Fort Collins, Colorado, shoots a 31-inch 2018, with a broadhead, out of a 66-pound bow at 30-1/2

inches...and that "ain't possible," I tell him. But his arrows fly beautifully, for him. I'll bet I couldn't shoot that arrow out of a 55-pound bow!

Recurves, for the most part, are not critical on arrow spine. You should be able to come up with a good shooting arrow with a minimum of difficulty.

One problem I see with matching arrows to a bow is in the fletching that's available. Arrows with vanes are not recommended. Any archery shop attendant who would sell a plastic feather to a beginner should be hanged by his own bowstring. And to compound the matter, a majority of the plastic feathers are straight fletched. An accomplished and knowledgeable shooter may be capable of setting up and using plastic feathers, but the average bowhunter is not. It seems to me that everyone who shoots them has problems with arrow flight...but always rushes to advise you that they are waterproof. I could cure 80 percent of the arrow flight problems in the world today by ripping off all the straight fletched plastic feathers and replacing them with real, helical fletched feathers. If I were you, I'd insist on nothing but arrows with helical fletched feathers. If your archery dealer won't/can't do them, find someone who will. A straight fletched arrow is an abomination. With a broadhead on the end it is difficult to shoot accurately under ideal conditions...under hunting conditions, they're a joke. You're needlessly penalizing yourself.

About the only other thing I do to set my bow up for hunting is to stick a couple pieces of yarn in the string to silence it.

One of the nice things about learning to tune your recurve is that once it's done...it's done. You probably won't have to mess with it again for years...unless you change something major. Don Morgan, a friend from northern Colorado, called me the other day and asked some questions about setting up this new bow he'd bought. "Couldn't remember how to do it," he said. It seems that Don's last bow purchase was over 20 years ago and he was still shooting it with the same string that he'd originally had a fellow in Denver make for it. Now, I admit that's unusual...but I've heard dozens of similar stories. As mentioned earlier, I've shot the same nock point setting since I started in archery.

On occasion, if I shoot a different bow, or put on a new string, I'll have to spend at least a full 10 minutes putting on a new nock point and finding the right brace height.

8

Occasionally even the best shooters miss—at such times saws are very handy.

Getting Better

"**O**h, no! Damn! I'll **never** have another chance like that!"

"Crap! That arrow is probably in Denver by now. Good Lord! It must have gone a foot and a half over his back. How could I have done that? He was right there...**right there!** Pick a spot? I did...Colorado! Didn't even get to full draw. I couldn't have done that...**couldn't** have...he was so close. I could have jumped out of the tree at him and come closer to killing him. Damn...damn...damn!"

Give or take a word or two, that little sequence of verbal self-flagellation could have fitted perfectly into a big percentage of the bowhunts taken last year...and could have been spoken by any one of about 50,000 bowhunters. They **couldn't** have missed that shot! Right?

They say it's one of the privileges of hunting with the bow and arrow...the right to miss. But, sometimes, for the life of me, I find little solace in that right. Sometimes, it's not so bad to miss...but mostly it's the blackest, most awful thing I can think of. It's one thing not to see animals and it's another thing to have the wind, or some such, mess you up. But, for me, when I've said, "Okay...I'm gonna drill this bugger...this is the one I've been waiting for"...then blow it all completely because I missed the shot...well, it's...it's just black-awful. I want to say, "Wait...hold everything...turn the clock back

...let me do that again." But, as you know, the gods of the hunt hate a whiner and they won't ever go back...no matter how hard you beg.

What's to be done about it? Get better. That's all I can offer. Get better at shooting. Get better at handling that quaking, gut-rending, breathless, brainless phenomenon known as "buck fever."

Get better. As near as I know, it's the only answer.

I have a theory. It is that if you practice a thing over and over and over, until it becomes completely ingrained into your physical and mental being, that often you will/can, under unbelievable pressure and distraction, perform that act without thought. I apply that theory particularly to shooting a bow. If you practice shooting a certain way, over and over and over until it becomes automatic...when things get rough, your instinctive memory takes over and can run your physical being without your help. In other words, if the bow shooting part of it is completely entrenched in you, and a big deer comes along and a bad case of buck fever takes over, you've got a much better chance of just instinctively doing the right things...without the assistance of your brain...which is usually going "uh...uh...uh."

I am a big advocate of shooting and practicing with your bow constantly. I believe shooting and practicing with your bow will help you be more successful in the woods. And, of course, that's because through practice you become a better shooter, but it's also because with the right kind of practice...which would be simulated hunting shots...you've put yourself into a quasi-hunting environment, which, I believe, in its fashion helps build a deja vu form of hunting and shooting experience. Meaning that when you are suddenly presented with the real life hunting situation, and it is just like the situations you've been practicing all the time, your body is saying, "I've done this before." And quite possibly, it'll do it just like it did in practice. Let's face it, for most people, there simply isn't enough hunting season or enough exposure to animals to always be calm, cool and collected when Mr. Big walks by. Practicing what you believe may actually happen in the woods...the kind of shot you might be presented with...can help. Believe me, it can.

I've wondered over the years why so little has been written about practicing with a hunting bow. Oh, in just about every big "here's how you bowhunt" book, there's a few lines about being sure you practice with your broadheads because they shoot differently. But there never seems to be much in-depth stuff. Maybe my concern has evolved because I'm encountering fewer and fewer bowhunters who actually do what I call bowhunting practice. In fact...and I lay it to today's modern equipment...I see fewer bowhunters shooting their bow than I can ever remember. And they say that's one of the reasons why people like that kind of equipment...because they don't have to practice as much. That's more than a bit sad to me. And that's not because they aren't practicing...it's because I see it as an erosion of bowhunting. Of course, it's my personal opinion, but I really think that shooting a bow and handling the equipment of our sport is part of the mental process of approaching a hunt. The less involvement there becomes with bowhunting's trappings, the more involvement we see with killing an animal. And thus, there's a preoccupation with success...and not with bowhunting itself. I know that lots of people disagree with that...and some will say that's the way it's supposed to be. But I see it happening...it's as plain as the nose on your face...and I don't think it's a good sign.

Practice with lifelike targets is a helpful bowhunting activity.

There is information available on practicing for tournaments. And, for sure, at any archery lane you can get all the free advice you can hold. But most everything is slanted toward hitting a bull's-eye. I think it is important that bowhunters understand that there is a very big difference between target practice and bowhunting practice. They are not the same. Don't misunderstand. I have all the respect in the world for target shooting. I personally do not have the talent to do it. And I also believe that a certain amount of shooting at paper targets with scoring rings on them is good for you because it puts a number to your skill. It gives you a barometer of just how good or bad you really are. But, continuous practice at paper targets is not the best way to practice for a bowhunt. Of course, there are target shooters who take their deer every year, but they are the exception and usually are persons who've spent a great deal of time target shooting **and** hunting.

Target shooting is static. Indoors, it is performed at known yardages under ideal conditions of light, temperature and terrain. Outdoors, it is only slightly less controlled. Bowhunting, on the other hand, is not static...and the yardage is never predictable. And certainly, it is rarely, if ever, performed under ideal conditions of light, temperature or terrain. The light is usually fading—or it's just barely getting light—the temperature is usually colder than you wished it was and the terrain is either uphill, downhill or worse.

With shooting a bow for hunting, we are only concerned with the first shot at a given target. In the woods there is only a single shot...it is always at an unknown yardage, with rarely an opportunity to readjust and recalculate. There is only the one chance...if you miss it, that's it. The season may be over for you.

The differences between shooting a bow at paper targets indoors and shooting a bow for hunting are like the differences between an accomplished playground free throw shooter and an NBA basketball player. The playground free throw shooter has time to bounce the ball a bit, take a few deep breaths, shake off the tension and shoot the ball with absolutely no interference. The NBA player must run up and down the floor, leap high in the air to shoot the ball and perhaps twist his body slightly in the process to avoid the outstretched hands of a seven-foot defensive man. He must make split-second decisions and have instant reflexes. Both shoot a basketball and use the hoop and wear short pants...not much else is the same. Tournament shooters and bowhunters both use bows and arrows...there are few other similarities.

There are many ways to practice for bowhunting. The two I use most are stump shooting or "roving" and shooting at animal silhouettes. There are other methods of practice, but they all seem to be variations of these two. I guess I do more stump shooting than anything else...but that's probably because it seems to fit me and my needs better and it's so easy to do, particularly in hunting camp, and there is literally nothing to set up or take down. Stump shooting isn't just shooting at stumps. Stump shooting is a broad, random sort of bowhunter's practice which amounts to wandering about and shooting arrows at whatever appeals to your eye. Your target can be practically anything. A leaf, a clump of weeds, a dead stump, a dark place on a tree trunk, or a shadow that looks like a browsing deer. Stump shooting can be done almost anywhere. An open field, a nearby woods, a drainage ditch, an area near your campsite...anywhere you won't be shooting at the same target over and over. The rules are simple: You never shoot more than a single arrow per person at any target and you must vary the distance each time to the next target . And, if there are two or more people, the one who made the closest shot chooses the next target.

You might start with a tall thistle a few yards away, waving slowly in the breeze. Retrieving your arrow, you make a fantastic shot on a shadow. And then you cut one loose at a wind driven leaf that moves uncertainly along the ground. A dead log is never passed up because it gives you the opportunity to pick one spot, on the whole, to shoot at...and that's important. Sometimes you swing, draw and shoot quickly. On the next shot try using the set-arm draw method...setting your bow arm straight at your target and then pulling it back slowly and shooting...like you would if a deer was very close and might see any movement. And so on. When two or three bowhunters get together for a little stump shooting, there's no end to the targets and the unorthodox shooting positions that can be thought up.

A few words about your practice equipment and clothing might be in order right here. You should do your practicing with the bow you intend to use for hunting. It should be set up as it will be for bowhunting. You're wasting your time if you do all your practicing during the summer with a 50-pound bow and then plan to jump to a 60-pounder just before the season. I know that people do it...but I don't think very many of them do it successfully. If you hunt with a bowquiver, put it on...and keep it on. A bowquiver can dramatically change the balance and the shooting characteristics of a bow, so it's best if you do all your practicing with it. If you're a camo bowsock lover, by all means keep it on during practice. I don't think it is important as to whether your bow is camo painted or not, or whether your string silencers are in the same place, because they don't seem to have any effect on shooting. But anything that will affect the way your bow shoots should be in place...all year.

Shooting broadheads is a problem in my neck of the woods because of the rocky terrain. Some fellas have to shoot them exclusively for the last week or two before the season, because their broadheads shoot so much differently. I don't, simply because I can't really say I can tell any difference between the flight of a field point, or a Judo, or a single blade Black Diamond Delta. Oh, I'll shoot my broadheads ...each one of them...before sharpening them to make sure everything is together properly and functioning as it should. But, I do a minimal amount of broadhead practice. I'm lucky, I guess, because it's a problem to get decent broadhead practice without a sandy bank someplace and no such creature exists in my part of the Rocky Mountains.

As for getting out there in all your hunting clothes and practicing, I would never consider taking a piece of clothing on a hunting trip until I've worn it during a practice session to make sure it fits right and doesn't interfere with my shooting. But, I don't wear my hunting clothes everytime I practice like some writers suggest. Our bow season here in Colorado comes in August/September and the temperatures are fairly mild. Normally a single layer of cotton or light wool clothing is all that is needed, so there's not the problem with layers and layers of clothing. I'm mostly just making sure I haven't outgrown them or that the tail end isn't torn out.

I remember running into this fellow one year high up in the Sangre de Cristo mountain range. I'd been hunting sheep for several days and it was the opening day of deer season. He was hunting deer. Well, it seems as though he'd packed his son's camouflage coveralls by mistake. Unfortunately, this year his son was away at college and wasn't with him...and home was several hours away. It made for a real problem because his son was about six inches shorter than dad...which made for a much shorter pair of coveralls...particularly from the crotch to the shoulders. But dad was convinced that you couldn't bowhunt without camouflage, so he wore them anyway...buttoned up all the way. I saw that poor man two or three times that weekend and he was always walking with his back bent over and his knees bent...trying to find a little relief in the crotch. Check your fit before opening morning.

Clothing for really cold weather is quite a different situation, however. And here I'm referring to temperatures that require layers of bulky clothing to stay in the woods any length of time. A couple

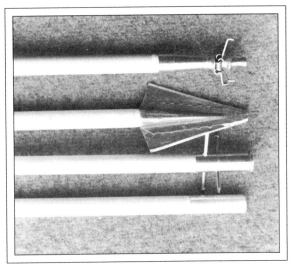

From top to bottom: Judo point, dubbed Black Diamond, .38 casing with nails, steel blunt.

of years ago I chased whitetails around in Nebraska when the temperature was 22 degrees below zero and the wind was blowing 16 mph. That's cold enough to give the proverbial brass monkey cause for concern. Granted, that's unusually cold and you could only stay out in it for a short time...but that was more because of the limit on the amount of clothing I could wear and still shoot my bow than it was on the temperature. Personally, I have a very difficult time shooting a bow in cold weather clothing. I can always find clothes to keep me warm, it's just not easy to find warm clothes in which I can shoot a bow. For that reason I am particularly selective about the cold weather clothing I use. I do quite a bit more testing and checking fit and such before a cold weather hunt. If you have a similar problem, you should do the same. Remember... you're practicing for hunting season...make it as realistic as you must.

As mentioned earlier, when I'm on a hunting trip, even if it's only a weekend sortie, I am shooting arrows off and on all the time when I'm not actually in the woods. During an early Colorado mule deer hunt, I'll shoot lots of arrows each day...not at one stretch, but a half-hour here, an hour there, etc. Sometimes I shoot at a 3-D animal silhouette but mostly I rove and stump shoot. Walk and shoot, walk and shoot. Sticking a Judo in my hip pocket, I'll take out across the sage flats, or up toward the sparse quaky patches on the side of a hill above camp, picking out this wildflower, or that patch of brush for a target as I go. It's a good time for me. Usually, between shots, I'm thinking about what I did wrong during the morning hunt and what I'm going to do this afternoon that will work better.

One year, in the Colorado high country, toward the end of what had been an unsuccessful attempt to nail a good muley, I was wandering about shooting at things and trying to figure out just what I was going to do about changing my lousy luck. I had wandered into a little creek bottom below camp and was shooting at little clumps of willow that grew here and there up and down the side of the bank. As I bent to retrieve an arrow, I saw a very nice deer bedded in the shade back up tight under a big clump of willow about 30 or 40 yards down the creek, but only about 10 or 15 yards up on the side of the bank. He must have thought he was hidden. I never looked straight at him. As cool as anything I shot another Judo down the creek ...this one as close as I dared to his hiding place. It was down in the bottom, near the water...a little past him, but still close enough. I could see him watching me as I strolled slowly toward my practice arrow. Thank God for bowquivers. As I walked, I pulled out an arrow with a broadhead and put it on the string. Out of the corner of my eye I could see he was nervous, but he wasn't leaving. I leaned over, like I was going to pick up the practice arrow and turned just slightly and shot him, right there...smack dab...still in his bed. Was he surprised! I felt almost evil...like it was almost too easy. That shot came so easy. I'd probably shot more than 50 arrows in the half hour before I shot him. Since then I've thought how much better I'd be if I could always do that...shoot a bunch of warm-up arrows before the big one. Now...we both know that wasn't one of your standard wise old bucks. But, to this day, I still keep an eye out for animals as I shoot. I've seen several while stump shooting, but that buck was the only one I've ever put a tag on.

I've found the Judo point hard to beat for stump shooting. They weigh about the same as my broadheads and seem to fly about the same. And best of all, they don't disappear under grass and leaves everytime you shoot them. The Judo point, which is made by Zwickey, may seem expensive, but it isn't really when you consider that they are practically indestructible and impossible to lose. I have a Judo point that has outlived at least 10 arrow shafts. You can make your own using a .38 caliber casing and small nails. They work pretty well. Steel blunts are the next best. They are inexpensive and don't burrow under the brush and grass too badly. Field points will work, but plan on losing a few. As mentioned earlier, it's hard to use broadheads where I live because of the rocky terrain, but if you can use them, you're a step ahead. A friend of mine does all his stump shooting with broadheads. He has a large pasture, which is randomly scattered with single bales of old straw. By varying his shots from bale to bale he can shoot broadheads, but not be restricted to the same shot constantly. If you know a friendly farmer who will let you wander through his fields after baling, you'll enjoy some realistic, challenging practice. The shape of the bales is similar to deer and you'll get practice at different angles...not just the too commonly depicted broadside deer shot. I wouldn't use broadheads, however, because there's too much danger of one coming off in a bale and ending up inside a cow's stomach. Judos work well and will only penetrate a few inches. Quite often they'll bounce off.

Try all types of unorthodox shots. Shoot under low hanging branches and through tiny openings in the brush. You'll be learning where you can and can't shoot...how an arrow acts when it leaves your bow...how high it arcs, how strong you have to be to shoot out of position and how much different things look when you do. Kneeling is different from standing to shoot. Many of my shots, when still-hunting, are from my knees...so I practice shooting off my knees a lot.

Let me toss in a little secret here...when shooting off your knees, it's a lot more stable and versatile to shoot off both knees...both knees on the ground. Putting only one knee on the ground, and bending your other knee and putting that foot along beside it is not nearly as solid. Plus, if you're on the wrong knee, you'll find it almost impossible to shoot to the opposite side, i.e., with your left knee and your right foot on the ground, it's almost impossible to turn to the right and shoot...but with both knees on the ground you can cover 180 degrees easily. Those are the kinds of things you learn if you do enough stump shooting.

Take a look at the kind of hunting you normally do, or the kind of shooting you're going to be doing on your big hunt this coming year, and try to practice your shots accordingly. Are your shots mostly from tree stands? Are you a stalker? Maybe you do a lot of both. If you're heading west, remember that the average shot on a western bowhunt will be longer than your typical tree stand shot in Alabama. There will also be less undergrowth and trees and that will make it harder to judge distances. Do as much stump shooting as you can in open country. Mule deer hunting in Wyoming calls for longer shooting, plus a lot of uphill and downhill angles. Say you're going on an antelope hunt in the west. Antelope hunting calls for some very different preparatory practice. You should ask your guide how the hunting will be done. More than likely it will be from blinds located near water holes. If such is the case, you need to practice shooting from within a very restrictive blind...through a small hole, at an animal that loves noisy bows (because they allow him to be running 40 miles per hour before your arrow is halfway close). Practice what you need.

Sometimes roving across the country stump shooting with a friend can be almost as much fun as hunting. It's a good chance for a little bowhunting camaraderie and the competition offered by another person can make it interesting. When I lived in Indiana, there was rarely a Saturday during the winter months that Bob Pitt and I were not out somewhere...wandering and shooting...looking for new hunting areas. It's a good way to do it. Look over some new country and shoot your bow. If one of us got to feeling a little cocky, there might be a wager or two laid. It was good fun. I don't do that as much as I used to and I miss it.

Shooting at animal silhouette targets is also excellent bowhunting practice, particularly if they are of the free-standing variety. There are some excellent targets available. Some of them are startlingly realistic. I wish I could get my hands on a bunch of three-dimensional foam targets. They would really be great for the bowhunter...but I've not seen any really good ones that are commercially made. I'm sure the cost of such an item would be prohibitive...particularly when you consider shipping costs. But if you're the industrious type, you can always make them. It's a lot of work but if good materials are used they'll take a lot of arrows for a lot of years.

At the Colorado Bowhunters Jamboree each year there are usually lots of handmade three-dimensional targets for shooting. One year there was a life-size bugling elk (with a real six by six rack attached, an appropriate bugling tape and a speaker nearby) that made your palms sweat just to be around it. That target probably had as many as 5,000 arrows shot into it every day for three days...and it was still in good shape the last time I saw it. But...that target was built by a half dozen ladies from an archery club in Ft. Collins...and I understand they worked on it for two weeks...not to mention the cost, which I'm sure was considerable. So...as I said, unless you're the industrious type, three-dimensional targets are only available at large, organized shooting events. But, such things are good things to attend and if you can keep your mind in the proper order, they are good bowhunting practice.

On a lifesize animal target you must pick a spot, just like when you're bowhunting.

The dense foam targets that have become available in the last few years impress me greatly. The targets from Perrine are as good as anything I've seen. While they are not really three-dimensional, they are painted so expertly that they appear almost real. And they are made to be free-standing, which I consider important. They will take thousands of shots...with field points. I am familiar with people who have been using one of these targets for years...and they show no indication of wearing out. Some do shoot broadheads at them, but my experience has been that they won't last nearly as long. You can put a few bucks into one of these things...but not huge dollars...and in the end, I think they are good investments.

It is preferable that your animal silhouette targets be free-standing. By free-standing I mean that they do not need to be attached to a back stop of some sort. Free-standing targets are much better for forcing the eye to judge yardage. If you put your silhouette on a target butt, your eye, within a shot or two, has the range and you lose the value of having to instinctively estimate yardage. If it's free-standing, you can move around a bit yourself and confuse your instinctive eye, or even better, you can move the target to another setting for each shooting session.

The best thing about shooting at animal silhouettes is that they teach you about picking a spot on the animal to shoot at. That is very important. For an instinctive shooter, the majority of his misses at animals will be because of a failure to pick one single little spot to shoot for. When you are shooting at animal silhouettes, you have a lifesize animal target in front of you and to do it right, you have to pick a spot. Lots of times, when you are stump shooting, you are shooting at complete things...like a leaf, or a small clump of grass...and are not picking a single spot on a larger object to hit. So, shooting at animal silhouettes fills a very basic need for bowhunters...the need to practice picking a spot.

But, as stump shooting's problem is that you aren't always being forced to pick a spot, silhouette shooting's problem is that, in a very short time, you are no longer shooting at unknown distances. No matter how much you move around and up and down, on each shot, your instinctive memory quickly puts a subconscious number to the thing based on relative size and too soon you might as well be shooting at a paper target with a bull's-eye.

Ideally, you should mix your stump shooting with shooting at animal silhouettes. One very good idea is to scatter a number of animal silhouettes across your stump shooting area. Vary the yardage and your shooting position on each shot. If you don't have enough foam silhouettes, you can make some from cardboard and staple them to sharpened strips of lathing pushed into the ground. You can just shoot through them and patch the holes with small bits of masking tape. The tape will hold the targets together for a lot of shooting and it will also cover up what would otherwise soon become an aiming point.

In the end, a bowhunter has to **want** to practice, I guess. There isn't much chance of a person doing enough of it if he doesn't want to. And, of course, one of the things that happens is that you need to practice to learn to shoot well...but there is a resistance among many bowhunters to practicing if they don't shoot well. So maybe, if you're one of those people, you just need to grit your teeth and practice like crazy...knowing that skill will come with practice...and then it'll be fun for you.

Nothing can take the place of practice. Not style...not equipment...not technique...and not all the natural ability in the world. If you won't practice, I'd as soon you didn't come into the woods. All of bowhunting would be better off if you stay home and watch TV.

9

Accuracy equals success.

Questions & Answers

What sort of accuracy can I expect shooting a recurve bow instinctively?

As with any bow, the recurve bow itself is capable of pinpoint accuracy. When the human factor is removed, the bow can be shot, I suppose, into a teacup at 200 yards...the point being, mechanically the bow is capable of far greater accuracy than anyone human can ever get from it. However, putting a bowhunter in charge of its accuracy brings the range somewhat closer.

Most instinctive shooters should limit their shots to 30-35 yards and under...and I think that is the upper side of it. I say that for this reason: when a deer is observed at ranges greater than 30-35 yards, it is difficult to pick a single spot because the eye is seeing the complete deer. The deer is far enough away that it is almost impossible **not** to see the whole deer and his silhouette...which, again, makes it difficult to pick a single spot on the animal. Now...if someone were to stick a red spot on that deer's vitals...some one thing to concentrate on...the whole situation changes. That is why instinctive shooters can often shoot very well at targets with aiming dots or at things like paper milk cartons at distances out to 100 yards...there is something specific to concentrate on...the spot on the target—and the complete milk carton—which are small enough to focus the attention.

As far as individual ability is concerned, a beginning instinctive shooter can, I believe, reach his potential within a couple of years. And, of course, progress depends largely on the amount of shooting done. If you're one of those who picks up his bow a week or a month before the season begins, you probably don't have much of a chance to be a decent instinctive shooter...certainly not in any time less than many years.

As far as accuracy within 30-35 yards is concerned, instinctive shooters can splinter nocks and shoot perfect ends right along with the best of them. But, as mentioned earlier, it is difficult for purely instinctive shooters to shoot arrow after arrow after arrow into a two-inch circle for two hours because of the degree of intense concentration required. So, what you'll see are good instinctive shooters who can shoot right along with the best target shooter, but for only, say, 10 arrows...maybe 50 arrows...but rarely for a complete tournament.

Instinctive shooting is a bow shooting method particularly suited to hunting. It can be developed to such a degree that your shooting becomes almost supernatural. You can learn to shoot dimes out of the air and to shoot running rabbits without thought. But it's unlikely that you'll be able to stand in one place and shoot a dime affixed to a target butt 40 times in a row, as some target shooters can do. And you'll probably have difficulty shooting a paper rabbit in the prescribed kill-zone 40 arrows in a row.

Should I be shooting wood arrows out of my new recurve bow?

You can shoot any arrow that is matched to the bow, be it wood, aluminum, fiberglass or some composite shaft. Recurve bows do not require the use of wood arrows. I shoot wood arrows because I like wood arrows, not specifically because I think they are better than, say, aluminum. Wood arrows can be as good as aluminum, and perhaps, in some instances, better...but, for the most part, wood arrows are not as straight, as consistent or as available as aluminum. But I love shooting them. I recommend that if you are new to recurve shooting, stay with aluminum until you have the shooting style and transition from compound to recurve under control. Don't throw too many variables into the pot. If you're not shooting well, you'll not know whether to blame the arrows or call the bow maker. Once everything is under control, if you feel the wood arrow calling, then do it.

I want to be able to shoot well enough to kill deer out to 60 yards. How much will I have to practice and how long will it take?

Wrong! Wrong! Wrong! Don't do it unless you're talking about shooting deer with a rifle. Deer, or for that matter, elephants, cannot be killed consistently at 60 yards by anyone shooting any kind of bow. First off, probably one in 50,000 bowhunters can hit a washtub at 60 yards and probably only one in a million can hit it every shot...which is when you get to consider taking a shot at an animal at that distance. And then there is the fact that an animal has time to move several feet forward (perhaps to grab a bite from another bush) during the time your arrow is in flight from 60 yards and what may have been a perfect shot becomes a gut hit. It is not responsible bowhunting...so forget it. Learn to kill them every single time at 20 and 30 yards. You'll be amazed at what that will do for your success ratio.

My new recurve shoots to the left all the time. What's wrong with it?

The bow is probably all right. It could be a center shot problem, which can be solved by matching the proper arrow with your bow. Remember, if your bow is not center shot, your arrow match-up becomes more critical. But with the correct arrow the bow will shoot fine. Shooting left can also be caused by arrows which are under-spined. There is a good chance that your problem is caused by leaning your head too far into the arrow as you shoot...which would move the tail of your arrow to the right, which will cause your arrow to shoot to the left. This is a fairly common problem with shooters who are switching from a compound to a recurve. The bow has a different feel; the let-off isn't there and so there is a tendency to lean out to meet the string. This is basically moving the rear sight to the right, which moves the front sight to the left. Visualize your arrow as a telephone pole. When you move the end in one direction, the other end points in the opposite direction. Remember (assuming correct arrow match-up) an arrow only goes where it is pointed.

Hand placement on the bow can also be a factor. Assuming you're a right-handed shooter, placing your hand too far "into" (or to the right of) the bow handle, physically moves the bow to the left, which will cause arrows to impact left. Again, if you're a

A summer's trophy from Pritchard Mountain.

78

new convert to recurves, the bow's draw weight may be a factor. The recurve is a different feel and often folks get too much hand onto the grip because they are stronger that way.

What size cedar arrows should I be shooting out of my 55-pound bow?

First off, keep in mind that there is no genuine, hard-and-fast rule that can be applied to come up with the exact arrow for a given shooter. That is, what you shoot and what I can shoot out of the same bow may vary somewhat. There is always some experimentation required for really fine tuning a bow. But, in most cases, I find that the following general rule works: add five pounds of arrow spine for each inch of arrow length over 28 inches, plus five additional pounds for a broadhead. So, if your bow is 55-pounds and you are pulling it 29 inches, I would suggest a minimum spine of 65 pounds (55 pounds **+** five pounds for one inch over 28 **+** five pounds for a broadhead **=** 65 pounds) For half-inch increments, I move it forward to the next inch and I normally throw in another five pounds of spine for longer draws. If you are pulling your 55-pound bow 30-1/2 inches, I would recommend 55 pounds **+** 20 for draw length (about 15 would be exact) **+** five for the broadhead. So, as you can see, it's a generally broad formula. But I've never known anyone who came up with an arrow that wouldn't shoot using it.

The most exacting way of coming up with the correct spine for you and your bow is to shoot all different spines of arrows and select the best one. Most folks simply don't have available to them the variety of quality wood arrows necessary for doing it in that manner. I have always hung to the heavy side on spine. My rule is, if you're going to err on arrow spine, do it to the high side. An overspined arrow will shoot fine...an underspined arrow won't shoot into the same place twice.

How do I get my bow quiet enough for hunting?

Brace height is a big factor in bow noise, although I guess I should say that individual shooting style/method is about as big. Your draw length, the way you hold the bow and the way you release, as well as the type release you utilize, will affect bow noise. A friend of mine who shoots a 64-inch bow, with bow quiver attached, shoots his bow at six and one-fourth inches of brace height and it's as quiet as a church mouse. When I shoot his bow, it rattles like a bean in a boxcar. I have to raise the brace height on his bow about another half-inch to quiet it to an acceptable level for me. Personal shooting style has a lot to do with how quiet your bow shoots. Generally speaking, the guys with the shorter draw lengths will shoot quieter than the guys with the yard and a half draw lengths. Proceed with changing the brace height slowly. That is, don't twist it up and then down a half-inch or three-quarters at a time. Brace height is more subtle than that. Take it a few twists at a time...restring it...and shoot it. In some bows you'll find that a six and three-fourths inch brace height is too noisy, and that six and seven-eighths sounds really good...but when you take a twist out of it and drop it back to six and thirteen-sixteenths you almost can't hear the bow at all...it's perfect. Point being, there is an exact brace height at which your bow will be quietest. Play around with it...particularly when you've got the time to do it and aren't rushing to get to your tree stand. I find it to be a nice midday diversion.

I can't see any difference between whether you shoot a tab or a glove, but there is a definite difference in noise level based on the amount of bite, or the depth of the hook you take on the string. Shooting off the very tips of the fingers is difficult to do well and therefore I don't recommend it...but it is quieter shooting. I personally would prefer shooting bare-fingered. It doesn't seem to bother the tips of my fingers, but eventually the underside of my top finger goes to pieces and I have to quit. I find that I shoot a bow considerably quieter when shooting bare-fingered. I'm not sure just exactly why that is...consider that with a really deep hook, the string may have to move as much as five-eighths of an inch to one side to escape your fingers. So, the deeper the hook on the string, the more string oscillation at the moment the shot is made...which is going to cause more noise.

I've never been able to properly quiet a bow without some sort of string silencer. I've put yarn in my string for years, although recently a friend gave me a few strips of beaver skin with the long hair attached...which seems to work as well and is definitely classier. There are a lot of string silencers on the market and I think all of them work in varying degrees. "Puffs" and "Catwhiskers" seem to be the most popular. The spacing of the string silencers does make a difference, so move them around a bit and experiment. If the bow requires it, I'll use more silencers as opposed to using bigger ones...a personal preference. I may put four small yarn silencers on the string...spaced appropriately...instead of using two really large wads. It may not be any better, I can't say for sure.

Some bowhunters put moleskin, or some such material, in the string groove to dampen the slap of the string on the limb. I use flemish spliced strings on my bows and the wax will sometimes make a small sound as it lifts from the surface of the limb, so I often put moleskin in the string groove for that reason.

Bow quivers and accessories are notorious rattlers and noisemakers. And I would add here that the more things you hang on your bow, the more noise it's going to make...or, perhaps more accurately, the more things you are going to have to quiet and worry about. Although it's a fact there is a point at which you can add enough physical weight with accessories that the bow will shoot quieter because the thing gets too heavy to vibrate and magnify sound. True story.

Bowquivers are the worst offenders...but they're also the best thing invented for carrying hunting arrows...so you need to learn to quiet them. A bowquiver must be securely and solidly mounted to your bow for hunting. It should hold your arrows securely and they should be spaced in the quiver so absolutely no feathers and none of your broadheads touch during the shooting process. Otherwise you're all but wasting your time trying to get and keep the thing quiet.

If you're having difficulty with your bowquiver try these steps:

1. Start by removing all arrows and hand tightening any nuts or bolts, including the attaching system to the bow. Hold the bow in your left hand and with your right hand, hit the quiver a few times to simulate the vibrating action of the bow when you shoot it. Do this without arrows in the quiver. Adjust, tighten, or pad whatever is necessary to get the bowquiver completely quiet in the empty state. If you can't quiet it when it's empty, throw it in the trash and go looking for another type that you can get quiet.

2. Once your bowquiver is completely quiet in the empty stage, begin adding a single arrow at a time...shooting it several times with the addition of each arrow. Be aware that screw-in points, either field or broadheads, are major noisemakers when they are slightly loose...they can be almost like tuning forks unless snug. If you allow the point of your arrow to come in contact with the top or the edge of the hood you'll discover another noise generator. Replaceable broadhead blades or

Preparation is the key to bowhunting success. Above, the author packs out the antlers of a big Colorado elk.

auxiliary blades for conventional broadheads can cause noise.

3. Add each arrow, one at a time, and shoot the bow several times to make sure it is still quiet.

Usually it's a fairly simple process of elimination to find and stifle whatever is making noise. Another point to be considered is that often when you add accessories to your bow you'll have to go back and raise your brace height a bit. Your bow may shoot quietly, without accessories, at six and one-fourth inches. But with bowquiver attached you'll have to raise it up to six and one-half inches. This is very common.

I'm getting a "clanking" or "clicking" sound when I shoot...what's going on?

Sounds like either an underspined arrow or your brace height is too low. More than likely, the latter. Take a couple of twists in the string and raise your brace height a little. It'll probably go away. The "clanking" you're hearing is being caused by the string interfering with the arrow paradox and causing the arrow to hit the side of the bow. Another indication of the same problem is a marked up arrow plate or rest, right at the point from which the arrow exits the bow. If raising the brace height doesn't solve the problem, go up five pounds or so on arrow spine. One of these two will end your problem.

It doesn't matter what arrows I shoot, they all go crazy when I shoot off the shelf. You said that wouldn't happen. What's wrong?

First off, you cannot shoot plastic vanes off the shelf. You didn't say, so I'll assume you're shooting feathers. The next question would be whether or not your bow **can** be shot off the shelf...a few production type bows on the market are very difficult to shoot off the shelf...and the manufacturer will tell you that they intend for you to shoot from an elevated rest. In such cases, it's a difficult situation. I'd either attack it with a file or buy another bow, myself. Nock point location is a key factor in good arrow flight from the shelf. A nock point set too low is the usual cause. I set mine at about one-half inch **above** 90 degrees. You may be

able to get by with something slightly lower, or you may need to go a bit higher. Remember, up and down arrow flight is normally caused by a nock point too low; left to right arrow flight is normally brace height.

I've been shooting a compound and want to switch to a recurve. How do I know what bow weight I should select...and what will be my draw length?

Let me answer the easier part first. Figure that your draw length will drop about one inch when switching from a compound to a recurve. I think if you use that as a general rule, you'll be very close 95 percent of the time. Selecting the right bow weight is not so clear cut. In the end, it's such a personal thing. Some individuals go from a compound to a recurve, shoot the same exact weight and have no problems. Those individuals are rare. Most bowhunters need to drop down in weight somewhat. Lean toward the lighter side. I think if I was going to state a general rule, it would be if you're new to the recurve bow, don't order one over 55 pounds. A 55-pound bow will shoot completely through about anything on this continent. Most male bowhunters can handle a 55-pound bow. A few can shoot bows in the 65-pound range accurately...but not very many.

When I first began shooting a bow, very few people shot anything over 45 pounds. Everyone shot, by today's standards, lightweight bows. Men's equipment was 40 to 50 pounds, with 40 to 42 being the most popular. It probably had something to do with the fact that most were field archers also...and tournament competition accuracy was the goal. My first bow, a 46-pounder, was a "heavy bow." A year later when I jumped to a 55-pound bow everyone was sure I'd lost it. With my draw length, I was probably shooting 60 pounds or over...insanity! In retrospect there is a lot to be said for lighter weight bows. By "lighter" I mean 40 to 60 pounds. A lot of today's bowhunters...and I'm speaking of traditional archers...could stand a little reduction in bow weight. It's a crazy syndrome bowhunters get into. I've been as guilty as anyone. Heavier and heavier. Ninety to 125 pounds...Lord! I think the sport would be better served if, instead of going up in bow weight, we issued T-shirts that the archer could wear stating for all to read, "My other bow is a 125-pounder." In that way they could strut and yet be able to shoot something they can draw without flushing the woods. The man who can slowly and smoothly draw and accurately shoot, straight down, a bow over 70 pounds, after standing immobile for four hours in 20 degree weather with 85 percent humidity off a tree limb 20 feet in the air, is exceptional. And that isn't a dreamed-up formula to test your strength...it's what you need to be able to do when hunting whitetails from an elevated stand. I've watched bowhunters go through the damndest roundhouse bunch of gyrations to draw their bows...I almost fall down laughing. I thought one guy was, at first, offering his bow skyward to the sun god before he started his draw. He threw his rear end to the right, his shoulders to the left, hooked his toes backward into the carpet and with eyes bulging and a great release of air, wrestled it back. Hunted with it, he said...Hmmmm. Under hunting conditions, there wouldn't have been an animal within 100 yards by the time he got to full draw. Reminded me of the preliminary movements of an Olympic weightlifter jerking a barbell off the floor. If you can't slowly, very slowly, pull your bow to full draw without jacking your bow arm skyward, you are overbowed. You've heard it a thousand times...shoot the heaviest bow you can handle, accurately. Understanding what "accurately" means may be the problem. And keep in mind, to achieve accuracy you really do need to be able to draw and shoot your bow, assuming you're shooting instinctively, without being aware of the effort of drawing the bow.

There isn't a thing wrong with hunting deer with a 45-pound bow...the sport would be better off if more tried it. And a 125-pound bow is fine also...if you can shoot it accurately. But use good judgment, not ego, for your decision. Shooting a bow should be fun...not a test of strength.

Keep in mind that you are going into something new. If you overbow yourself, you'll probably never be able to shoot the bow accurately and you've wasted your money. If you go lighter, you may a year later say..."I could have gone a couple of

pounds heavier on this bow." That's fine...nothing has been hurt and you've probably learned to shoot the recurve quicker and more accurately than if you'd start out heavier. You can order your next bow a few pounds heavier. Arrow flight and sharp broadheads are more important to good penetration than bow weight.

Which is best, three-fletch or four-fletch?

I would say that the correct answer depends on the individual shooter. For some, three five-inch feathers are enough to stabilize their arrow. Others, myself included, need more feather. Feathers are what straighten and stabilize your arrow when you shoot. Some guys get off the string clean enough that they can even shoot four and one-half-inch three-fletch. As stated earlier, arrow flight is the key to good penetration, so you want your arrow to straighten up as quickly as possible. More feather surface can accomplish that. It can also make your arrow noisier in flight and increase its trajectory (slow down the arrow). I would add as a point of interest, however, that arrow maker Pat Graham, whom I consider to be as knowledgeable as anyone in the world on wood arrows, claims that his testing with a chronograph showed that four-fletched arrows were quicker through the chronograph than were three-fletched arrows. I would assume that is because they are straightening up quicker and thus not losing as much speed during paradox as the three-fletch. Now, that is chronographing the arrows within a few feet out of the bow. I feel fairly certain that the three-fletched arrow will catch and pass the four-fletch out at about 20 yards or so...For me, the four-fletch straightens up quicker, but I like the looks and traditional aspect of the three-fletch better...ain't that a bunch of raspberries? I shoot both. With the three-fletch, I shoot a big five and one-half-inch feather.

What is the most important thing when shooting instinctively?

I consider the bow arm the most important thing in instinctive shooting. It does the initial pointing at your target; it is also the end of the barrel where the bullet comes out and it plays a major role in the quality of your release. I sort of talked around this earlier, but, when I'm shooting poorly...arrows wandering all over, etc...I try to focus all my attention onto my bow arm. **Push**...I tell myself. Concentrate on that target and push with that bow arm. When I get that part of it right, the rest of it will **always**...every single time...fall into place. It could be a little different for you...but I doubt it.

My old compound must have weighed a ton. The recurve I bought is so nice and light, but I can't shoot it worth a damn. The guy at the archery lane said my new bow is "too light." Is that true?

There is a lot of truth to what he is saying...that is, a bow can be "too light" (here we're talking physical weight, not draw weight). However, I can't say for sure that your poor shooting is for that reason without watching you shoot. But, regardless, to pursue this physical weight thing...I feel that an amount of physical weight in a bow is desirable. It is certainly nice to walk through the woods with a bow in your hand that weighs nine ounces, but my experience has been that a really lightweight bow is harder to shoot. Let me give you an example: If you were to hold a feather in your left hand (arm's length, palm up) and a can of peas in the right hand, you'd find that it is much easier to hold the can of peas in your right hand steadier. Reason? The can

of peas weighs considerably more than the feather and thus offers more resistance to your "holding" effort. Try it. I know from personal experience that if your bow arm is wandering all over, and your arrows are getting farther and farther apart, that you can steady your wandering arm and tighten your groups by adding physical weight to your bow. Again, the added weight offers resistance to the bow arm and allows it to move less as you aim.

However, one arrives at a point in this weight thing where the bow can end up being uncomfortably heavy. On a target line, a physically heavy bow is not a problem (in fact, it's probably an asset to shooting a higher score). Climbing a mountain in Colorado, or even finding your way to your stand in the dark across three barbed wire fences and a half frozen creek, with a bow that weighs as much as a machine gun can be a real problem. Some like and perhaps need more physical weight in their bow than others. I personally prefer something over one and one-half pounds but less than two and one-half pounds. I think it has a great deal to do with the quality of your bow arm. If you happen to be one of those fortunate ones with a good, steady bow arm you can get by with less, I believe.

Try adding a little weight to your bow...perhaps a bowquiver...and see what happens.

10

"Either you like wood arrows or you don't; it's that simple."

Handcrafting Wood Arrows

There aren't a lot of things more pleasurable than building wood arrows. It pleases me partly, I guess, because there are few things of importance remaining in our sport that can be done by hand, and probably a big part of it is because it seems to be capable of immersing me, body and soul, up to my armpits, in the witchery of the bow and arrow.

Wood arrows by hand are part of my barrier against technological encroachment...a hiding place for hunting instincts that refuse to be stirred by blister packs and Velcro® and screw-in this and that. And nothing, not a single thing, smells like Port Orford cedar. Even when they're broken you don't want to throw cedar arrows away. I find pieces of wood arrows in my pockets, in my duffel...on the kitchen table...just wait, you'll see. It is strange really...other kinds of arrows get tossed or thrown into a pile to be straightened at some time that never comes. Why is it that wood...? Aaah, I wrote about all this before, didn't I? You either like wood arrows or you don't...it's that simple.

If you do like them, at some time in your bowhunting career you'll likely fall off the deep end...much as I have...and feel the need to try your own hand at building them. And if you do have a feel for them, you really should indulge that feeling and try your hand at building them.

Certainly, beautiful, well-matched wood arrows can be bought. I buy and shoot tapered woods from a custom arrowmaker regularly. But the satisfaction of building and shooting the product of your own efforts is something you'll not find for sale...not at any price.

Yes, it is time consuming to build your own arrows. Yes, the equipment to do it will cost you some money...but then doesn't everything you do to amuse or entertain yourself? No, you do not need to be a builder of custom guitars to do it, and it'll not take more than a few dozen before you can call yourself capable. Listen, if I can do it...

I was lucky, I guess, because right off I bought a fletching jig. I'm not sure why exactly, because I am, above all, not a "do-it-yourselfer." I am without talent. I once made a birdhouse that hung vacant for two years...birds wouldn't touch it. I took it down out of humiliation. If I remember correctly, a fellow named Jim Van Ness, who was the first archer I met, said I had to have a fletcher and know how to build my own arrows. So I did it. I ordered a "kit" for building my own arrows from the Kittredge Bow Hut. There was a fletcher, a dozen nocks, 36 feathers, and a "how-to-do-it" booklet. The points and the feather burner had to be purchased separately. I did my first dozen on the dining room table. They were dipped full length orange, and had three gray barred feathers and a white nock. They were beautiful.

First off, you must have arrow shafting. You can, if you're convinced you **are** going to do it on a grand scale, order direct from one of the shaft manufacturers. Or, if you're a bit timid about the whole thing, you can buy a dozen or two from your local archery dealer. In truth, however, unless you go directly to one of the custom arrow manufacturers who will sell you matched raw shafts...which you'll pay dearly for...it is unlikely that the shafts you'll get will be matched close enough for any kind of quality wood arrow.

So, the problem, almost before you've started, is that unless you already own the equipment to spine and weigh the shafts you purchase, you will end up with a less than acceptable arrow unless you buy from someone who has spined, weighed, and matched the shafts. Maybe the custom arrow maker is the better idea.

Wherever you procure your shafting, remember that the quality of the shafting is paramount to building good arrows. Buy the best you can afford.

Types of Wood Shafting

With the renewed popularity of the wood arrow, a number of shafting types have appeared/reappeared. While 95% of the available wood shafting is parallel Port Orford cedar, there are several other choices in varying degrees of availability.

There are tapered shafts, footed shafts, compressed cedar shafts, and a variety of others such as fir, birch and larch. The tapered shaft is a parallel shaft which has eight to 10 inches of the nock end tapered from 23/64 to 5/16 inches, the theory being improvements in flight characteristics and reduced feather wear. To my eye, the claims definitely have merit, as the tapered shaft does seem to recover quicker and shoot somewhat better than the regular parallel shaft.

The footed shaft is made by inserting a piece of hardwood in the business end of the shaft to increase shaft strength and durability. Footing was very popular in the early days of our sport. I've only owned a single dozen of them. The theory of

durability does make sense, but the ones I owned were of such poor overall quality that I could never determine much about them. It would seem to make for a tip-heavy arrow, I would think.

The compressed shaft has been around off and on for many years. While I haven't seen what is available today, as I understood the process in the '60s, a cedar block was compressed under pressure and then dowelled into shafting. The result was an extremely durable and heavy wood shaft of smaller diameter (5/16 of an inch, I believe). The heavier shaft in the small diameter was said to produce an arrow with particularly good penetrating characteristics. The prices I've heard for the compressed shaft, while perhaps supportable, were mind boggling beyond the gasp range.

There are also a number of what I'll call specialty materials being offering on a limited basis. Woods such as hickory, fir, birch, are available in small quantities from a couple of sources. While these materials can be turned into good shootable arrows, their supply seems very limited, and I'd not recommend them right off for the novice arrow builder.

Tools of the arrow-making trade.

How to Order Shafting

The key factors are the spine and grain weight of the shafting. Spine, at least enough of it, is the most important single element for arrow performance. Spine is the term of measurement for stiffness of arrow shafting. It is measured by using a weight to depress the arrow shaft while suspended between two points. The amount of bend determines spine. My experience has been that with a center shot bow the key is getting enough spine. Within reason, too much spine seems to make little difference. It seems that if I need an arrow spined at 60 pounds, there is no way a 50 pound shaft will shoot properly. But a 65 pound or even an 80 pound shaft will shoot fine. For that reason I recommend that if you have any question about what spine is right for you, lean toward the heavy side. Keep in mind, however, that as you go up in arrow spine...which is strength...the arrow shaft gets more dense and generally heavier. So, don't go overboard on the heavy side.

With bows which are not center-shot...particularly longbows...it is much more important that the shaft be properly matched to the bow. With non-center shot bows the arrow is being forced to encounter the arrow paradox more acutely and the arrow's spine is much more critical to bow performance.

However, no matter what you've been told or what you've heard or read, what will shoot well for me and what will shoot well for you, out of the same bow, at the same draw, may vary tremendously. I know a bowhunter who shoots a 60 pound bow and uses a 60 pound shaft. I shoot between 65 and 70 pounds and nothing less than 85 pounds, preferably 90 pounds, will work for me. Draw length, bow weight, arrow release, bow setup, and who knows what else affects what works best for you. Shoot what works.

So...what do you order if you've not had the experience of wood? A decent rule of thumb is to take your bow weight, add five additional pounds of spine for each inch of draw over 28 inches and then add five more for the broadhead. For example, consider a 50 pound bow at 28 inches being pulled 29 inches. Start with 50 pounds, add five pounds for

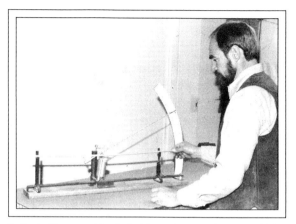

Bulk shafting must be tested for spine; results vary widely.

the 29 inch draw (10 pounds if it was a 30 inch draw) and then tack on another five pounds for the broadhead. That calls for 60 pound shafts (and I'd personally fudge another five pounds into it to be on the safe side) for that 50 pound bow.

From a physical weight standpoint it is most assuredly your choice. Wood shafts can be located in just about any weight you prefer. Maybe you should select a weight that corresponds to your current arrows. That way you'll have a good comparison of performance.

Spining and Weighing

If you bought your shafts spined, weighed and matched, you're ready to start the finishing process. If you didn't, that is, if you bought bulk shafting either from the manufacturer or a dealer, you're a long distance from the finishing process. You are going to need a spine tester and a grain scale. To my knowledge, there is only one spine tester on today's market. Don Adams of Elmira, Oregon offers one. If you can find one of the older ones gathering dust somewhere, that'll work fine also. I have a Scheib Spine-O-Matic from yesteryear. It's pretty fancy, but the Adams spine tester works as well and is sold at a fraction of the price. Use of the spine tester is simple. Follow the instructions closely.

Use a grain scale to weigh each shaft.

You'll notice right off that you get different readings when you turn the shaft so the grain is horizontal and when it is running vertical. Be consistent. Spine all shafts with the grain, which is the direction in which they are going to be working against the bow's sight window. I use a color coding system for segregating the various spine values. Using felt tip markers, mark each shaft as you spine it; i.e., red is 60/65 pounds, green 65/70 pounds, etc.

Once you've spined all the shafts, sit down and let the shock wear off. The broad range of spines you have before you may vary as much as 30 or 40 pounds. It's not unusual. But you're only halfway through. Each spine group now must be weighed and broken down further. You need a grain scale for this. Martin Archery offers one. It is a good one and is fairly inexpensive. I have a balance beam scale that is made by RCBS for reloading shells. It is very accurate but very slow to use. If you have to buy one, I'd lean toward the one from Martin. As I weigh each shaft, I write the weight on each with a soft lead pencil. Write at the top near your spine color coding. It will be cut off when you do the nock taper.

Depending on the number of raw shafts you purchased, you'll see before you a comparable number of small groups of arrow shafts...right?

You're beginning to see why custom arrow makers charge so much for matched shafts. As I recall, the last 1000 shaft lot we purchased took about 30 hours total time to spine and weigh. Ah well, what else of importance would you be doing on those cold winter nights? And TV will turn you into a toad anyway.

Picking and Choosing

Setting aside the spine group you intend for yourself, start batching the grain weights together in 10 grain groups. I rubber band them together. You'll notice that while your grain weight through the total batch varied 100 to 150 grains, within each spine group the weight range is much less. I find that a raw shaft weighing 430 grains will produce a completed 30 inch arrow of about 600 grains. That's with point, nock, feather and a coat of stain and clear sealant. However, when I cap and crest that same arrow, the physical weight jumps to 650 to 660 grains. As you can see, paint adds considerable weight to the arrow. On the other hand, once you have a feel for the thing, you can produce an arrow that will weigh just what you want it to.

Anyway, back to picking and choosing. Look for straight tight grain in the shaft. They'll be the straightest and least likely to warp. Some shafts will be perfectly straight the first time you pick them up...others will jump out of your hand when you spin them across your thumbnail. Select the ones that weigh the closest and seem the straightest. Keep in mind the wood shaft that is naturally straight is an oddity. For the most part, you'll have to straighten them all.

How to Straighten Wood Shafts

Remember, all wood arrows have a tendency to warp slightly with changes in humidity and temperature. You'll need to check each arrow periodically. My experience has been that each shaft should be continually straightened during the manufacturing process. I may go through a batch of shafts I'm about to begin work on as many as 10 times, each time hand straightening each shaft as needed. I'll do this over a period of seven to 10 days.

All this is done **before** work begins on them.

After a few straightenings, if an arrow is going to be usable for serious stuff, it will pretty well begin staying straight. The shaft that keeps going back to its original crooked state time and again goes to the rabbit arrow pile.

The easiest and most accurate method of straightening wood shafts is (if you're right handed) bending the crooked area in the opposite direction around the base of your left thumb while manipulating the opposite end with your right thumb and forefinger. With practice it will become a simple, quick task. Pat Graham, who once owned a custom arrow business, can hand straighten a wood shaft to perfection in seconds. That same shaft might take me several minutes.

Some suggest warming the crooked portion of the shaft over a hot plate or by briskly rubbing a rag over it. When the shaft is warm to the touch, it is straightened. This supposedly "sets" the shaft as it is straightened. I've discussed this with several arrow manufacturers...all have tried it, and all report negligble differences with or without the heat.

Some roll the shafts across a smooth flat surface to help detect crooked areas. I've seen this done quite a bit. However, it does seem to me that the overall straightness of the shaft is better detected by spinning across the thumbnail and by sighting down the shaft.

Tapering the Shaft for Nocks

Now is the time to taper the shaft for the nock. For your beginning efforts I'd suggest one of the little plastic handheld tools. They are getting difficult to find so you may want to take a look at the motorized disc sander from Arrow Dynamics of Ft. Collins, Colorado. It's the best I've seen. While the hand-held tools will work, there are limits to the accuracy you can expect to achieve. I think the cutting of the nock—and particularly the broadhead taper—to be extremely important. Let me explain. My theory is that before any tapering, the shaft must be as straight as possible. For several years I bought raw shafts from a fellow because he had a production type tapering machine. I'd receive my order tapered and cut to length. Ready for painting and fletching. Come broadhead time I'd find that half to three quarters of my arrows shot horribly...even though parts of the same batch had shot admirably with field points and blunts. I decided his tapering machine was out of whack and eventually took my business elsewhere.

It wasn't the machine's fault. I continued to have the same problem until Pat Graham set me straight. And this is perhaps one of the keys to making good shooting wood arrows...everytime. All shafts are straightened...as good as you can do it...**before** any tapering is done. Read that sentence again. Think about this. If you taper your raw shaft before it is straightened...keep in mind that the tapering process utilizes the shaft as the basis for setting the taper straight on either end...the taper might well be put on at an odd angle because the shaft it is working off of is at an odd angle also. If you've put the taper on without straightening, when you **do** straighten the arrow, the taper, in most cases, is now crooked in relation to the shaft. Simple, isn't it?

The shaft must be as straight as possible before any tapering is done.

I felt like a real bonehead. My experience since has been that if I follow the procedure of straightening and then tapering, that no matter how warped and crooked the shaft becomes it will still shoot broadheads straight. My theory is that the tapers are in line with the forward thrust of the arrow and even though the shaft in between is crooked, the guidance is on the proper plane. I know that as sure as you make a blanket statement someone comes along and blows the raspberries at you, but I can say that since I began following this procedure, I have yet to build a single wood arrow that won't shoot a broadhead. At this stage in the process I only taper the nock end of the shaft.

Finishing Process

At this point you are ready to either dip the shaft full length—whether you prefer color or the clear—or to stain the shaft for a darker look. I prefer the stained shaft. It "snaps" the grain of the shaft and makes a better looking arrow to me. If you prefer dipping full length without the staining, skip over the staining process and go on.

Staining

Wet a rag or paper towel with your choice of wipe-on/wipe-off stains. There are hundreds of colors and types available. It should be an oil base for best results. Each shaft is completely wet from end to end with stain and set aside for a few minutes. Before the stain begins to dry, wipe the excess off with a clean rag. Do not allow the stain to dry before you can remove the excess. You'll have a poor looking blotchy finish and also an unacceptable gummy surface. When wiped clean, the stain that remains has soaked into the grain and seems to leave no residue on the wood surface to create adhesion problems. It is advisable to use rubber gloves for the staining process.

Dipping the Shaft

For this operation you'll need a dip tank of some sort. The Bohning Company makes a couple of good ones. Your archery dealer can get them for you, or you can make your own from polyethylene or aluminum tubing (PVC will not work). Stopper them

with corks. Keep in mind that the larger the diameter of your dip tank, the more paint it will take to fill it, conversely, a tube too small will require replenishing the paint after every two or three shafts. I've been using two or two and one-half inch irrigation pipe. It's very inexpensive.

There are many good grades of lacquer on the

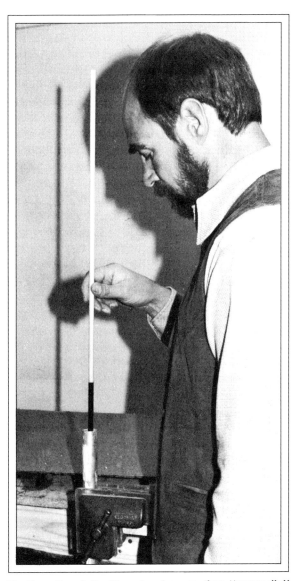

Dip the entire shaft with a clear lacquer, then "crown dip" if you wish.

market. You can experiment with them and find something that pleases you or you can shortcut the laboratory work and buy all your finishing materials from the Bohning Company. Bohning specializes in arrow building and finishing systems and unless you simply prefer to cut your own trail I'd suggest using their materials initially. The colors and options they have available will boggle your mind. Your local archery shop should be able to help you with any of the Bohning products.

I start by dipping the complete shaft, end to end, with a clear lacquer. In my case this is going to seal the entire stained shaft. Because of the stain, it seems that a single dip seals the shaft adequately. Without the stain, I dip the shaft at least twice. It is recommended that the second coat be applied while the first is still damp. Better coat-to-coat adhesion is claimed.

Thin the finish, if necessary, with the thinner recommended by the paint manufacturer. Some thinners and paints are not compatible, so don't just grab the first can of thinner you see. Buy twice as much thinner as paint and do it/order it all at the same time. When the dip tank has been filled with paint you'll notice lots of tiny air bubbles on the surface of the finish. Allow the tank to stand until all bubbles have come to the surface. Lifting the tank slightly and tapping it lightly on the floor a couple of times will hasten the bubbles to the surface. If your mixture is too thick the air bubbles will not dissipate. Either skim the air bubbles off the surface or pop them with a pin as they appear. The few bubbles that appear as you dip the shaft should run off. The consistency of the paint should allow the excess to run off the shaft freely in a continuous flow.

Dip the shaft and remove it rapidly, holding it above the tank until the excess flow is reduced to drops. Then hang it to dry. I hold the shaft with a clothes pin and then utilize it as a hanger. The drying rack is a piece of one-by-two inch furring strip, suspended between the backs of two chairs, with finishing nails driven in every inch. The clothes pins hang nicely on these.

Air temperature and humidity are important.

Lacquers should not be dipped at temperatures below 70 degrees. The paint should be room temperature. Working when the humidity is above 45 degrees is not recommended.

Allow the shafts to dry overnight.

If you do not intend to cap (also called crown dipping) or crest your creations, you are ready to begin the fletching process. If you've lost your nerve, your patience or your creative desires have begun to wane, skip the next part and go on to fletching.

Capping and Cresting

Capping is the 10 inches or so of (usually) colored dip that is put on the nock end of the shaft under the fletching. Cresting is the small colored bands just below the feathers. Cresting, I am told, was originally a means of identifying the arrow's owner. Mostly, it is just fancy pants stuff these days. Capping and cresting are the Sunday clothing of the arrow making art. It's a final personal touch in a sport overflowing with the look-alike sameness of woodland camo and face paint. Speak up bowhunter...individualize yourself.

However, besides just being fanciful, capping and cresting can be helpful in making your arrow visible in flight and for hit identification. For me, those are important items. I went the camo arrow route one year. I might as well have been shooting a rifle...only the bang was missing. When I turned loose of the string it was like shooting in an unlighted root cellar. The arrow disappeared. If the animal fell dead within view, I only experienced a few seconds of panic...of not knowing what had happened. I did not like that at all. Besides the need to identify a hit on an animal, I came to the realization that seeing that arrow in flight is part of the lure of this sport. Something is very definitely missing when I shoot and see nothing at all.

Many wood arrow makers crest their arrows but do not dip them. A couple of bright colored bands can do wonders for an arrow. Actually, the forefathers of our sport only crested their arrows. I'm guessing, but I'd imagine capping arrows probably didn't become popular until the heydays

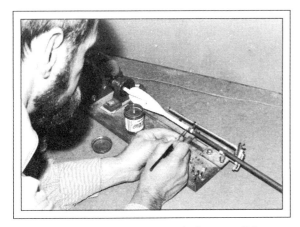

Cresting an arrow creates a custom look you can't buy.

of field archery in the '40s and '50s. Okay. Capping arrows. Mark each arrow shaft with a soft lead pencil so the depth of your caps will be identical. A cap about nine or 10 inches is standard, although a shorter one of six or so inches looks fine. Don't worry about the pencil line; it will be covered by the cresting. I use a smaller dip tube for capping. Mine is about 10 inches long. Air bubbles are a bigger problem when capping because they will be more visible on the colored cap than they were on the clear dip. Try to get them all out if you can.

All capping begins with a thin white base coat...no matter what color you intend your arrows to be. The white provides an opaque base which will allow you to cover the shaft with one or two dippings. Before I knew this trick, I once dipped a red aluminum shaft nine times with a yellow cap before it covered the red. After nine passes the cap was about 1/32 inches thick and looked as if I'd pulled a piece of yellow garden hose over the end of my arrow. Anyway, a single coat of white is the answer. Since white is used on all arrows, I set aside a dip tube solely for this purpose. Again, the consistency of the paint is important. It should be thick enough to cover well but thin enough for the excess paint to run off the end of the shaft before it sets up. Check the first shaft you cap closely to make sure there are no waves in the finish near the nock taper. Two

or more thin coats are better than a single thick coat. Use the same dipping procedure for capping...dip and remove the shaft rapidly, allow the excess paint to run back into the dip tube...when the run-off is reduced to drips only, repeat the process. Hang to dry.

Installing the Nock

Test the fit between the nock taper and the nock itself. Sometimes, if your paint was a bit thick, you'll have to remove a small blob of paint from the end of the nock taper. A sharp knife or a coarse piece of sandpaper will do the trick. IMPORTANT: With wood arrows, nock placement is key. The nock should be aligned so the nock slot is across the grain of the shaft. Look carefully at each shaft **before** you apply the glue. Once you've established the grain direction, apply a small amount of glue to the shaft rotate the nock on the taper as you seat it firmly. Check alignment of the nock and shaft and set it aside to dry.

The reason for the nock being positioned across the arrow grain, is twofold. First, it will position your shaft so the grain is against the side of the bow. This means the arrow paradox will be against the strongest part of the shaft. This is particularly important if you are shooting marginally spined arrows. And second, by always positioning the nock across the grain your final product will have a consistency of spine and performance that random nock alignment does not. I know one custom arrow manufacturer who argues that nock alignment across the grain is unimportant. His theory, and I agree with him to a degree, is that there is generally only two or three pounds of spine difference between cross grain and with the grain in quality arrows, and that small amount should make little difference. Agreed, two or three pounds of spine is not much...but I think I can see it when the nocks are randomly located. So, right or wrong, aligning the nock across the grain doesn't take over two seconds per shaft...so I do it.

Cresting

Up to this point you've probably been watching the progress you're making and perhaps thought,

'Hmmmm...no resemblance whatsoever to the custom arrows I've seen." I think the same thing...everytime...until I get them crested. Then I **know** it was worthwhile. Cresting is the fun part...because now you can really begin to see what your efforts have produced.

You'll need a crester. Bohning Company has two models. Either will work nicely. If you've a little bit of talent you can put one together yourself from any small motor which turns between 150 and 500 RPMs. My first effort was a variable speed hand mixer with a piece of surgical tubing between the motor drive and the nock. I used a couple of V-blocks to support the shaft. Some people are skilled enough to crest while rotating the shaft with the flat of the palm with the shaft supported by V-blocks. That might challenge my coordination to its limit.

The secrets of cresting are good brushes and paint consistency. The paint should be as thin as possible, but it should cover well. You'll have to experiment. Again, Bohning is a good source for cresting paints. Their products are all compatible one to another. They list various colors of cresting paint in their catalogue.

Keep your brush wet with plenty of paint so brush marks flow together. Work as quickly as possible on each band to prevent drying. Put all the bands of each color on all the arrows before going to the next color. Vary the brush size with the size of the stripe being painted. A good rule of thumb is something about one-third smaller than the stripe.

The tendency at first is to do too much cresting. My first creations looked like barber poles. You'll probably find that, like many things, the simple crest is often the most attractive. The best thing is to have access to several different arrows that have been crested. Once you look at a few, you'll have all kinds of ideas. For example, a small crest under the feathers adds a professional touch you'll not find anywhere except on handmade arrows. A small band between the nock and the feathers is pretty snappy also. And of course, nothing snaps a crest like silver and gold separating pin stripes. By the time you've finished your first dozen you'll have 200 ideas for your next dozen.

To keep my crest from smearing when the arrow

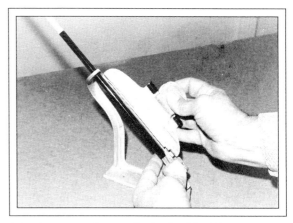

Take time as you learn to fletch. Good fletching is a key to arrow flight.

is being shot, I've started spraying a thin coat of clear finish over the crest.

Fletching

We're on the downhill side now...just minutes away from the finished product. Is your mouth dry? Are your palms sweaty?

There are several fletchers on the market, with most of them coming in a number of variations. I'm only familiar with the Bitzenberger and the Multi-Fletcher. I'm sure all the others work well. The Bitzenberger, I'd have to say, is the most precise fletcher available. It is also the simplest to use and the easiest to get consistent results with. The Multi-Fletcher also does a good job. It definitely can be adjusted to put more helical on your arrow than any other. It is probably a little trickier to operate than is the Bitzenberger. However, when I say easier or harder to operate, we aren't talking engineering degree required...we're talking about whether it will take a six-year-old child 10 minutes or 15 minutes to figure it out on their own. So, don't be concerned about difficulty. Putting feathers on arrows is as simple as anything ever gets in archery. The big plus for the Multi-Fletcher is that it will do six arrows at once. The Bitzenberger works better on the coffee table in the living room in front of the TV.

In choosing a fletcher you'll note the choice of clamp styles...straight, right or left wing. Some prefer straight fletching...it can be angled slightly for an offset effect. My personal theory is that an arrow needs to be helically fletched. Right or left wing makes no difference. The clamp you choose will determine the feather you will have to use. Left wing feathers seem more available in my area. Right wing might be more available in yours.

Die cut feathers are simpler and cleaner to use than are full length feathers. I find the die cut shapes that are available to my liking. One of the advantages of die cut feathers is that you can replace a single feather and have it be exactly the same as the rest of the arrow (an almost impossible task if you cut and trim full length feathers). I am seeing, however, that many bowhunters who are experimenting with wood arrows want to get as near the origins of our sport as they can. Many are opting for burning their own feather shapes. The use of full length feathers will necessitate the use of a hot-wire feather trimmer, and a wife who is minus her olfactory nerves. The smell of burning turkey feathers is one you'll not soon forget. You'll be reminded of it every time you enter the house for days on end. There are a couple of hot-wire trimmers on the market.

Whether you use parabolic or shield shaped feathers is a matter of personal preference. Parabolic seems to shoot quieter. Compatibility of your fletching cement with the paint on your shaft is something you need to think about. Oft times there is enough adhesion that you believe all is well...until it rains or until the arrow sees a little rough treatment. Be sure. I know a very famous bowhunter who dipped, crested and fletched up a brand new batch of aluminum shafts...paid $400.00 for a plane ticket...and went whitetail hunting in Indiana. He was found mid-morning of the first day back in his sleeping bag in the tent. Thrown in the corner was his bow with a bowquiver full of beautifully dipped and crested but featherless arrows. He remained in bed the rest of the hunt and refused to talk about the matter at all...and still will not acknowledge that it happened. Later we were able to locate the route he'd taken that first misty morning by the yellow and black feathers. The tree he'd stood in was easy to locate also...there were more feathers there. A good way to avoid this sort of thing is to use only products that are meant to be used together.

The size feather to use is partly a personal preference, but it is also a matter of personal necessity. I need a lot of feather. Others get good arrow flight with less. There are many things involved. It seems that arrow length, release, broadhead size and weight, and bow set-up all play a role. For some, the size of their fletching is felt to be a direct reflection on their abilities as an archer and bowhunter, and they'll change whatever they have to change to shoot the size fletching they think they should. That's okay. I believe that good arrow flight is the most important factor in penetration. So, I use lots of feather toward that end. If I can see anything other than a ball of color going straight toward the target...at anytime in the shooting process...I am dissatisfied. For the most part, I'd say three, five-inch feathers are minimal. Use what works for you.

Go slowly with your initial fletching efforts. Take the arrow out of the fletcher after each feather is affixed and look it over carefully. Do this until they are all satisfactory to you. Is the feather firmly seated on the shaft? Hold it up...can you see light between the feather base and the shaft? If you can, you're not getting the feather seated properly. As you insert the feather into the clamp leave a little space between the feather base and the clamp. That will give the feather base the flexibility to follow the shaft surface as opposed to the clamp surface. Be sure each end of the feather is firmly seated. Allow at least 15 minutes for the glue to dry on each feather before going to the next. Apply a small drop of glue to the top and bottom of each feather to seal them. As you can see, it's a simple operation really. You'll have it completely under control in short order. That's all there is to fletching.

Broadhead Tapering

I do my broadhead tapering at this point. It could have been done just as easily at any point after the full length dipping. My only concern is that the broadhead taper not be covered with paint. Many will disagree with that, feeling that covering the taper further seals it against moisture. I agree with that. I just find that the paint does not give the kind of bond with hot-melt glue that I want. And the painted surface is more uneven than is the raw taper...which gives me broadhead mounting problems. Yes, I know, the nock taper is covered with paint. I just don't consider it as important.

The same requirements apply for both the nock and the broadhead taper as far as straightness is concerned. Although, again, I consider straightness more important for the broadhead taper than for the nock taper. However, if indeed, a good straight grained shaft is being utilized, the shaft should still be as perfect as it was when you installed the nock. Nevertheless, I still check the straightness.

Make the broadhead taper as long as you can, or should I say as long as is necessary to reach the bottom of the ferrule of your broadhead. The more taper you can get inside the broadhead, the more strength you'll have. There is a limit to the length of the taper possible when using a handheld tool. With the disc sander I can adjust for any broadhead.

Point Installation

Use hot melt glue for the points, being careful not to scorch the wood taper as you apply heat. I use a propane torch to soften the glue and smear a liberal amount on the taper. It will set up quickly. Holding the point with pliers, I heat it and slip it over the glue on the taper. It will immediately re-soften the glue and allow you to seat the point firmly. Keep a container of water at hand to cool the point as soon as you're satisfied that it's mounted properly.

Broadheads are a different matter, of course. Sometimes they go on perfectly...more often than not you'll have to rotate them first one way, then another. I keep a small piece of plexiglas handy and use it as a smooth spinning surface. Standing the arrow on the broadhead tip, I spin it and observe its trueness. If you've straightened your shaft well before you tapered it, your problems with mounting broadheads should be minimal.

Well, there they are...your very own creation. A totally customized arrow...and you did it. Lean it up against something where you can get back and look at it. Hey...you did one hell of a fine job. "Store boughts" sure don't look like or feel like this...do they? The problem is...now they're too pretty to shoot. Guess you'll have to just make some more...

Part 2

Bowhunting Adventures

Photo by Judd Cooney

"It was a buck I heard coming through the leaves. . ."

11

A successful reunion hunt.

Reunion Hunt

This probably wasn't a very good idea to begin with. Not that going back to Indiana to hunt whitetails isn't always good. . .but trying to make it work in three days seems sort of dumb.

We'd started trying to plan a hunt clear back in September, but first one thing and then another had delayed it. Finally I just said to hell with business and got on a plane. Mostly it was just important that I came. I suspect if I could only have come for two days—maybe even a single day—I'd have done it. That **is** probably strange, I guess. Particularly when you're talking about whitetail hunting in Indiana. The whitetail capitol it ain't. There are no great numbers of big deer in Indiana. There aren't even great numbers of small deer. Although certainly there are adequate numbers and there **is** the odd keeper-type deer. Mostly it's only an average deer state. But. . .it is the one I grew up in. . .it is the one I hunted first. . .it is where I shot my first whitetail. . .and it is where my friend Bob Pitt lives.

Bob and I have ridden a lot of rivers and sat around a lot of campfires together. When I migrated to Colorado a few years ago we sort of figured we'd slowly lose contact. But it never worked out that way. The friendship remained. Neither of us have been in very many hunting camps without the other. So, actually coming back to hunt whitetails in Indiana is sorta like going back to a high school reunion where you get to hunt deer. No bad combination.

Actually, at this moment, I had bigger problems than worrying about how dumb a three-day hunt for whitetail was. A more pressing problem, at the moment, was just how I was going to make it through the first day. My head felt like a sponge. It hadn't been a very intelligent evening. We'd stood around in the Indianapolis airport for a long time waiting for my luggage and finally went upstairs to the lounge to wait there. That started the whole thing. Then on the way to Bob's house we'd stopped to see a couple of people. And then a couple more. By the time we'd finally gotten to his place it was pretty late. Then we'd gone down to the basement. We shouldn't have done that. That is where all the hunting paraphernalia and deer horns are kept.

I have an uncommon—and perhaps unhealthy—interest in hunting paraphernalia and deer horns. Bob probably has the world's greatest collection. Sometime later, much later, we'd said to hell with it. . .there wasn't any point in going to bed. We'd continued pilferring through the hunting equipment and playing show and tell. Actually, we'd had to hurry a bit at the last moment to get my gear sorted and ready to go hunting.

It was about 3:30 a.m. when we went outside to load the truck. It was going to be pretty nippy out there come daylight. But at the time the cold air felt very good. I'd started to fade a bit about a half hour earlier when all the loud talking slowed as we finished organizing our hunting gear. By the time we backed out of the driveway we were both a little numb, wishing we'd had sense enough to go to bed back before we'd decided not to. Ah well, we'd both done lots of crazier things and they'd all seemed like the thing to do at the moment.

We pulled into an all night restaurant just before we cleared the city lights and grabbed a couple of cups of coffee in styrofoam cups, as much to occupy ourselves as anything. Then we turned south down toward Owen County.

About 45 minutes later, a little over halfway, we stopped and got out in the cold to walk around and wake up. Then we were okay. Owen County was my old stomping grounds. I'd shot my first decent whitetail there a lot of years ago. That was pleasant to think about. I had been lucky, although at the time I'd thought differently. Well, this morning was going to be my chance to relive history.

Sometime during the previous evening we'd decided on this place. Bob had already hunted for three weeks and had a half-dozen places in mind, but he thought this one looked probably as good as any. Besides, it was fairly close and if we didn't do any good here, there were other spots within an hour or so that looked as good. Three days wasn't a lot of time. I tried not to think about the times I'd hunted Indiana for three days and not **seen** a deer. Of course, I told myself, that was years ago and it wasn't unusual then to only see a single deer during the whole 30-day season. There were lots more deer now.

When Bob turned off the gravel road and started back the dirt lane we'd always parked in, it seemed for a moment like we'd turned the clock back a lot of years. Nothing looked really different. It could easily have been 1968 again. The corn was just like I remembered it, the first four or five rows picked and the rest still standing. The lane looked a little more used than I remembered, but then weren't we all? I wondered if that corn picker was the same one, parked in the same place at the end of the lane, that we'd always parked beside. It probably was.

Bob was saying something and when I looked over at him he was looking at me with that look that said he had asked a question and was waiting for an answer.

"What?"

"Wake up," Bob chided. "I said we've got to hurry. It'll be light in another hour and we've got a long way to go. Can you find that tree from here in the dark?"

"I don't know. I guess so." I said.

"All you've gotta do is go to the creek and go down it to the railroad tracks and then you'll know where you are, right?"

I was trying to get my pack on and my bow strung.

"Yeah, I think so," I said.

"If you want me to, I'll take you."

Suddenly I felt very embarrassed.

"No, no. I'll find it okay. I'm just a little groggy right now. When we get up to the second field I'll get my bearings."

By the time we'd gotten everything all together and the truck locked I was shivering all over. The sign on the bank in the last little town we came through said it was 13 degrees. Lord. Thirteen degrees in Indiana's moist air feels colder than 10 degrees below zero in Colorado. I can never get enough clothes on when I'm back here. But once we started moving I'd be okay, I told myself.

"C'mon, I'm freezing."

Bob was checking all the zippers on his pack and all the buttons on his shirt pockets. He's a very orderly person. Meanwhile my teeth were beginning to make clicking noises as he rechecked the doors to make sure they were locked. Then we were off.

"I think I'll go get in that little water oak that you used to hunt in the bottom across the creek," Bob said. "So we might as well stay together 'til we get to the creek."

It had been three or four years since I'd hunted here and I wasn't sure I remembered just where the "little water oak" was, but I nodded agreement anyway.

The frosted brome grass in the field made it easy to see where we were going in the moonlight and we walked fast toward the creek. Within a few minutes I could feel the warmth returning to my arms. We learned long ago that putting all your hunting gear on and then walking to your stand didn't work. By the time you arrive, you're soaking wet with perspiration and half an hour later you're freezing. Instead, we walk to our stand wearing only pants, shirt and shoes. . .no long johns, no jacket and usually no hat. All the warm stuff is in our packs. It goes on after we get to our stand and have cooled down. It works unbelievably well. Generally, the time it takes to strip and redress cools you just enough that you don't sweat anymore, but there's enough heat in your body to keep you toasty for several hours.

Once we crossed the second field I had my bearings and felt sure I could walk to the tree in the dark with no problems. At the creek we talked in whispered tones and agreed that Bob would come to my stand at noon. With only three days to hunt, we'd probably go someplace else if these spots didn't look good. Bob hadn't been in here for over a week, so it wasn't impossible that it had cooled off a bit. I walked down the creek to the place I used to always cross. In the moonlight I picked my way across and felt pleased with myself for not getting my feet wet. A couple of hundred yards down the creek I turned south at the little drain and followed it until it disappeared and then I went up and over the ridge to where I could see the bend in the railroad tracks just ahead. From this spot the rails bend back south again and in the moonlight I could see the tracks for a long way before they disappeared in the dark.

Once I was hunting this place and was watching a small buck when a train came roaring and rattling past. The deer hardly looked up, even though the noise was deafening.

The ridge line turned east and took me back away from the tracks and in a few more minutes it widened out and the ridge disappeared. Slowing, now, I started watching the skyline, looking for the tree I was sure was nearby. I stood for a few minutes and tried to remember exactly where it was. To my left I think. Ah ha, right here. Old Daniel Boone had nothing on me. . .walked right to the hummer, in the dark no less.

Dropping my pack on the ground I unzipped the outer pocket and removed the pouch with the tree steps. I thought about how many times I'd done this under this tree. At least a half-dozen I'm sure, maybe more. It's an easy tree to stand comfortably in, so I decided to change clothes after I climbed up. Plenty of time before shooting light. . .and besides, I always hate to spend too much time on the ground around my stand.

Once I was in the tree it seemed it might have been a better idea to change my clothes on the ground. I'd forgotten how tricky it can be to stand on one foot on a tree limb that's covered with frost, while pulling on my long johns. . .in the dark. Getting my boots off and then back on is the worst part. Getting everything ready took a lot longer than it should. . .but then it was the first day and I'd not done this since last year and my brain and my body were running a little slow this morning. I was sort of dreading the long vigil. Normally I enjoy the waiting. . .but I figured today it was going to be a battle to stay awake. The cold would help some. But it would be awhile before it came creeping up from my toes. At least there was no wind. Just thinking about not going to bed last night made me feel droopy. As the morning eased out the dark, the birds began to make their short bursts of flight from bush to bush and I forced myself to be alert. Even though I've not taken very many deer at first light I always expect to. Mostly I see deer later in the morning...9:00 to noon sort of thing...9:30 to 10:30 is the hottest for me. It must have something to do with the places I choose for my stand. Others see more deer earlier, or later. As I recalled, the last deer I saw from this place came late. It was a buck that I heard coming through the leaves toward me just as I was starting to climb down right at dark. I waited for a minute and he came under me. You always think you'll be able to see them in the gray light, but you never can. I only knew it was a buck because I saw a flash of antler in the dimness.

Daylight came. About 8:00 a young six-pointer came soundlessly out of the little locust thicket behind me. He stopped under me for a moment, looked back the way he'd come and then hurried away to the north. He wasn't very big and I didn't give any serious thought toward shooting at him until he was gone. Maybe I should have thought about it. Only three days I reminded myself, not enough time to be selective. By 9:00 the day had begun to warm nicely. Standing there in the sun felt good, but it wasn't very healthy. Twice my legs buckled as I dozed off. The thought of the crippling effects of the sudden stop at the end of the 10 foot fall to the ground kept me awake if not alert.

Just before 11:00 I thought I heard a deer back to the east. Then a few minutes later, I heard it again. It was coming from sort of behind me to my right. When I heard it for the third time, I turned in the tree and faced that direction. It was getting pretty late for much activity. About 15 minutes later the sound came again and this time I could see a patch of deer hair down through the trees about 75 to 100 yards away. In a minute the patch of hair moved a little more and I could see that it was a good buck. He was at least a hundred yards away and looked to be moving in a line that was about parallel to me. Nice deer. I could see him most of the time now down through the trees. He appeared to be mostly just wandering slowly along, stopping every few steps to nose in the leaves for acorns. His main beam was so long that each time he bent down for an acorn it dug into the leaves. That was probably the sounds I'd been hearing. Very nice deer.

In the manner of feeding deer, he'd walk this way a few steps for a bit and then that way for a few more. Each time he'd turn in my direction, my heart would pound a little faster thinking maybe he was going to come my way. It did look like his general direction was beginning to change a little however. C'mon, gods of the hunt!

Slowly he continued to feed and move a few feet and then feed again and move again. There was no question now that he was beginning to bear in my direction. If he continued the way he was turned now he'd pass within maybe 40 or 50 yards.

Tempting, but still too far for my tastes. My brain was running a hundred miles an hour. Maybe, if he. . .can I? What if? Just maybe!

I kept trying to watch the buck and yet watch out ahead of him and try to figure where he'd most likely come. If he'd angle just a little more he'd come barely within shooting distance. He seemed in no hurry, which was certainly in my favor. However, even if he came close enough, it didn't look like there was any way I could get an arrow through that tangle of limbs and brush. From my stand 10 feet up I would have to shoot through half the trees in the woods. I'd not planned on doing any shooting back this direction. There was a little opening out there though. . .maybe. . .just maybe, he would feed into it. Still there was no way to shoot even there.

Stepping up on the next tree limb, I stretched up a bit and could see a little better. Hmmm. Maybe. Holding my bow in one hand I climbed up a couple more feet in the tree. That improved things a lot. Now I could get a clear shot if he fed into that opening. It looked for sure like he would now. I twisted off a couple of small branches as quietly as possible. Maybe a little far but he'd be broadside and 30 or 35 yards wasn't really all that bad. Now if he'd just hurry a little. This wasn't the best footing I'd ever had.

Beautiful deer. He was just easing into the opening, head down, searching for acorns. Just a few more steps. . .about right there. He stopped, raised his head and looked things over for a long moment. I didn't move a muscle. He lowered his head as though he was going back to feeding and then. . .plop. . .he laid down. No, no. . .not now! Damn. . .the bugger had bedded down. Damn, damn. . .about three feet shy of where I needed him and about two feet lower than where I could shoot. Now there were at least two thousand limbs between us. Great, just great. From where he lay bedded, he was looking directly at me. What now, great gods of the hunt? Here was probably the best buck I'd seen, at the very fringe of my shooting range, in a spot that an arrow could never penetrate. . .looking straight at me. . .and, of all the things to forget, Bob would be showing up pretty soon. Wonderful!

Photo by Judd Cooney

It was about 11:15 now...another 45 minutes. Unless Bob shot something or was having as much trouble staying awake as I had been and decided to come a little early. He'd be coming from the wrong direction, too. That would push the buck out of his bed and away from me.

Hey, maybe if I moved slow enough and could ease back to the crotch where I'd originally stood I would have a shot from there. Good idea. But it looked like he was staring directly at me. I might not move a foot before he spotted me. Like a sloth I ever so slowly began my move, trying to keep the trunk of the tree between me and the deer. Slowly...foot down to the next limb...one hand down...slower! Now another foot...slowly, slowly. I didn't take my eyes off the buck. He lay there looking straight at me but there was no indication he'd seen anything. Maybe I was really above his line of sight up here. I hoped so.

Slowly I made it back down to my original spot. Crap! This was twice as bad! I almost couldn't see him from here. Half past eleven. The countdown was underway. What could I lose? I began climbing back up the tree. Now I was moving a little faster. There just wasn't much time before Bob would come tramping up from behind me. Going up was easier and I could stay behind the trunk of the tree better. But I still couldn't understand why the deer hadn't seen all this movement only 35 or so yards away. Slowly I climbed past the spot I'd been before and on up the tree. I was wishing I'd chosen a bigger tree. These limbs were getting smaller than my wrist. And while that's not too bad in a maple, the ones above me were looking smaller and smaller. Still no sign of concern from the deer. Well, nothing ventured, nothing gained. I climbed higher.

I supposed I was 30 to 35 feet above the ground. Broken necks heal slow, I reminded myself. I thought maybe I could see a place that might be about half an opening down through the limbs toward the buck. A little higher. Hey, this was getting a little spooky. I could feel the whole top of the tree swaying from side to side as I moved higher. I tried not to put too much weight on any one limb. I'd felt the last one bend under my foot. Almost. No, still not quite enough room to get one

through. A little higher maybe. I was wondering if maybe I'd found myself a blind buck.

I knew the top of this tree was moving a lot. I could feel it. Ha, maybe the deer **could** see me and figured I was just a very big fox squirrel. Well, one more limb and that was it unless I moved out on the limb, away from the trunk. There was almost a shot here. Maybe if I just slid out a little from the trunk. There! A hole. Well, almost. By bending my knees a little it looked like I could maybe shoot. There was one limb about 10 feet out in front of me that was still in the way. I moved a few more inches out on the limb. Man, this thing was bending a bunch. As the limb bent under my weight, my shooting hole kept improving. I thought I could get one through now. Turning loose of the other limb I was holding on to and balancing on the one I was standing on was the next problem. Just do it, I told myself, don't think about it, just do it. I could feel the whole top of the tree swaying as I balanced myself, picked a spot on the bedded animal, came to full draw, tried not to look too much at the limb I wanted to miss...and shot. Clink! Bing! Thud!

Damn...guess I didn't miss that limb. I could see my arrow sticking in a tree that was three feet straight in front of the bedded buck (who was still there). It was sticking there, 10 feet off the ground. I could see the buck's eyes. They were twice normal size, trying to see everything at the same time. I could see him gathering his hind legs under himself...but he wasn't moving just yet. He was like a coiled spring, ready to go but not sure just where...just yet!

He couldn't see the arrow. It was sticking in the tree straight in front of him and it was too high and on the opposite side of the tree trunk. He'd heard the whole thing and he sure knew something was wrong. I had another arrow on the string. If he stood up I'd have a clear shot.

One second...two seconds. I could almost see him quivering with anticipation. I was ready. The coiled spring exploded. He didn't stand up. He didn't jump up. He literally came out of his bed in a single explosion that carried him 10 feet into cover. He hit, took one short bound and froze. He stood looking back over his shoulder in my direction, still not knowing what was going on, but sure he wanted no part of it. I slid another foot or so out on the limb. There was about a six-inch hole I could maybe get an arrow through, way out there. If I hit the hole, the arrow had to hit the deer square behind the shoulder...if I missed the hole, I missed the deer. There was no time. I shot. It was the best shot I ever remember making. He took a half dozen steps ...not leaps, steps, and collapsed. Lord! I was stunned.

The sound of shuffling leaves came to me and then Bob came walking up under the tree. Tilting his head way back and looking up at me, he said, "What the hell are you doing clear up there?"

He sure looked small way down there.

"Deer hunting," I said with a grin.

I started climbing down the tree. *How crazy can hunting get.* I wondered. The tree limbs I'd been standing on were hardly bigger than my thumb, the trunk was no bigger than my wrist. The whole tree was swaying and jerking as I made my descent. Under normal circumstances, on the bravest day I ever had, you couldn't get me up this high in this tree, I knew that. When I threw my bow out on the ground and jumped down, Bob was still looking at me kind of funny.

"You crazy SOB, what were you doing in the top of the tree?"

"Deer hunting, I told you. C'mon, let's go look at my deer."

"Really? Are you kidding me? Where is he? A big one?"

"Yep...not two minutes ago. He's right over there."

"All right!"

We walked over to the fallen deer. He was a decent animal, not terribly heavy antlered but he had a good main beam and nice long points...a good deer. I told Bob the story. He just shook his head and grinned. He was as pleased as I was. He always feels that he's responsible for getting me a deer when I come to hunt with him. He's not, of course, and we've talked about that. But he still feels it.

The pressure was certainly off now. I'd not seriously planned on doing anything other than maybe just have a chance to shoot a deer...and if I was lucky, maybe something with horns. But this...holy mackerel! A half day of hunting!

"Hey, how do you feel about laying down out there in the sun and taking about an eight-hour nap?"

"Sounds like a hell of an idea to me," Bob said, "You're probably tired after all that tree climbing."

Author's Note

This bowhunt took place in 1973 and today I certainly don't suggest anyone emulate my tree climbing practices. Use a safety line and remember that no whitetail buck is worth a fall and severe—perhaps fatal—injury.

Reprinted from **Bowhunter Magazine**, August/September, 1982

12

''When sheep hunting gets a hold on you, almost everything else takes a back seat.''

Bighorn Bowhunt

I wondered what time it was. I'd almost lost track of all time. For two days now, whatever ailment I'd contacted had kept me inside my tent, flat on my back. I'd slept so long I felt drugged. Except for the emergency dashes outside everytime I ate or drank anything, I'd done nothing but sleep and stare at the tent walls.

Great timing. The end of Colorado's bighorn sheep season was rapidly approaching and here I lay—invalid. I was as weak as a newborn baby, mostly from not eating. But every time I'd try, it wouldn't stay down. I was glad I was up here by myself; I'd have been terribly embarrassed for anyone else to witness my condition.

I certainly didn't plan my sheep hunt like this. I'd figured to spend the early part of the bow season hunting mule deer and elk. After that I'd still have a week or so of sheep season left. I figured to have the mountains to myself then. That part had worked out. The deer and elk hunting had been good and the sheep mountains were deserted...and I'd been seeing sheep. And then along came the black plague and put the monkey wrench to everything. I told myself by tomorrow I'd be okay and be able to get on with the sheep hunting.

I lay there thinking about sheep hunting. This was my seventh sheep hunt. All but one of them had been for bighorn sheep in Colorado. I'd gone to Alaska last August after Dall sheep. That had really been a fiasco. Better to think about bighorns in Colorado, although I certainly couldn't say I'd done any better on them. I'd hunted them better...more professionally, at least. But I still had never taken one. But then, I told myself, you only get to shoot one in a lifetime in Colorado...so you tend to look them over pretty carefully before you consider loosing an arrow at one.

There had been a number of sheep I could have shot at, but for one reason or another, I hadn't. That wasn't quite true. I did take a shot the first year I hunted sheep. Fact is, it was the first day...probably the first hour of the hunt. Wouldn't that have been something...had I not missed the shot? If I'd had any idea this thing would have taken all these years I might have reconsidered at some point along the way. Unlikely. When sheep hunting gets a hold on you, almost everything else takes a back seat.

It had always seemed like success was lurking just around the corner. Except for the hunt down in Beaver Creek in 1975 after I came back from British Columbia. That had been a mistake. Like a rookie, I'd put in for a permit in that area based on a discussion with a Department of Wildlife employee. He convinced me that Beaver Creek was the place to take a really good bighorn ram. I drew a permit there and had never set foot near the place.

Foolishness! Beaver Creek was a deep rock-walled canyon several miles long that was more like desert bighorn country than anything else. The midday sun scorched your body and the serviceberry and sage tore your clothes. Luckily the rattlesnakes and I missed one another, but the cactus had me watching the ground more than the canyon walls. It was dangerous to hunt with less than a quart of water and then you had to plan on being able to get more during the day. The tiny creek in the bottom, which gave the place its name, was the only source of water. I didn't see a ram in 10 days...and I was sure I wouldn't see one if I'd stayed for another 20 days.

Forgetting Beaver Creek, each sheep hunt had been a repetition of the one the previous year. I always had a good ram or two located by the end of July, but by the time the hunting season began, the last minute scouters and the backpackers had them pushed into the trees. I'd never spent less than 10 days hunting them and one year I'd hunted sheep for 23 straight days. Sheep hunting in Colorado isn't like Jack O'Connor said it would be. The first week of the season was when 90 percent of the sheep hunting took place and that week usually convinced the sheep that staying in the trees was the way to survive. It was unusual to find one up in the tundra again before mid-October—which was two weeks after the season closed. Going into the trees after them is as close to impossible as anything can be. They are three times as difficult to locate and stalk under those circumstances as are elk or deer.

This year I'd decided to hunt the Buffalo Peaks area. The season here was longer and I'd be able to wait until the tail end of it in hopes that most of the hunters would have long since given up and the animals would be back above timberline. So far, it appeared to be working. I'd found two rams with my spotting scope in a basin just above the edge of the timber the first evening after I'd packed in and set up my camp. It was too late to attempt a stalk that evening so I'd spent the last hour of daylight studying the terrain near them, plotting my stalk should they be in the same spot the next morning. That night the temperature dropped drastically and by morning the wind was gusting 20 or 30 miles an hour. The wind chill factor must have

been near zero. Not ideal conditions for shooting arrows at sheep on open hillsides. By noon it might be 60 degrees and dead calm or it might be worse than it was now. Weather in sheep country is like that. I was numb with cold by the time it was light enough to see. I was almost glad the rams weren't visible from where I sat—I was anxious to get moving and get some body heat generated. If the rams were still in this basin they were down on the other side of one of the finger-like ridges that ran up out of the trees. Twenty rams could easily be hidden down behind one of them. And it was certainly possible that they had moved into the trees out of the wind. The only way to get a better look was to circle around to the south and climb to the top of the mountain. From there I would be looking down into the ridges and cuts.

By the time I'd climbed to the top, the day had started to warm and the wind had calmed a bit. From the top I could only see a small portion of the moutainside below and so I had to keep walking slowly downhill, stopping to glass as more of the terrain became visible. I'd finally located a single ram bedded near the bottom of a cut against the base of a rock outcropping. Only the back of his head and horns were visible from this angle, but I was pretty sure he was a legal three-quarter curl.

I sat and watched him for a long time, trying to get a better look at him, but he wouldn't turn for a side view. Most rams look pretty good from a straight-away rear view. I decided to move closer just in case he turned out to be a good ram.

By flattening out on my stomach, I knew I would be completely out of his line of sight in the event he turned or stood during my stalk. Pushing my bow ahead of me, I slid down the mountain on my stomach to a spot behind some rocks 100 yards above the ram. It was close to an hour before the ram stood and began feeding down toward the trees 300 yards below. He was a typical Buffalo Peaks ram. Just barely three-quarter curl with heavy bases but thinning quickly after the first quarter length. It made no difference that I decided to look further, because the wind began blowing across the back of my neck. After standing rock still for another 10 minutes staring back toward me, the ram turned and trotted into the trees below.

That had been two-and-one-half days ago. I'd begun feeling poorly shortly thereafter. Within an hour I knew something had me in its grip and I headed for camp. By the time I arrived I was having to stop and lie down every 200 to 300 yards. I thought it would go away by morning. By morning it was worse.

Now, I was still hoping I'd feel better the next morning, except two such mornings had already passed. Perhaps I was going to have to load up and get out of here until I recovered. I thought about that for awhile and decided that perhaps my best bet was to get off this mountain and get to a doctor. Whatever was wrong with me could surely be fixed with medication. It sure wasn't getting any better laying here. If I went another day without eating I might have trouble packing myself and my gear out.

Okay, I decided, let's do it. By the time the tent was struck and my Kelty loaded, the worst was over and I started toward the trail I'd followed up from my Blazer three days ago. The walk was all downhill and I only needed to stop twice. For some reason I felt relieved when I finally saw my beat-up old green rig parked at the end of the trailhead. But then I started feeling like a quitter as I drove toward civilization. I told myself it's okay to be sick and it's okay to leave sheep camp to go to a doctor. But I remained unconvinced.

In town I located a doctor who was willing to see me in five minutes. It took me 15 minutes to find his office. Half the streets in town were unmarked and I finally had to ask a gas station attendant. As doctors go, he was a friendly sort who seemed to know instantly what was wrong with me. He said something had destroyed the bacteria in my stomach and that was why nothing would stay there. All I had to do was eat a little yogurt or buttermilk and I'd be cured. He commented that without something to form bacteria in my system again that I probably could have laid in that tent on the mountain until Christmas and not have improved. It all sounded too simple, but I was willing to try anything.

A stop at the grocery provided me with yogurt. The doctor said one cup would be enough. I badly wanted to be cured so I bought six. Three cups later everything was still okay and I decided to head back to the trailhead. I thought about heading back into the mountains but decided I'd best stay down here overnight just in case I wasn't cured. I figured to cook some food on the tailgate and sleep in the back of the truck. If everything seemed okay in the morning I'd head back in. This was working out better than I'd thought it would.

There was still plenty of light so I figured I'd best see if I could still pull my bow. We'd been doing a little experimenting back at the Bighorn Bowhunting Company and I had a new bow to play around with on this hunt. I was surprised I could still pull it. It was a 60-inch Bighorn Grand Slam—a little over 70 pounds at my draw. I shot a few practice arrows into a dirt bank. There was no question I was weaker but I felt sure I'd have no trouble when it came down to shooting at an animal. Well, anyway, everything was looking brighter than it had for a couple of days. I felt sure the food was going to stay put and I could tell I was feeling stronger already.

It was still two hours before daylight as I finished adjusting my pack, took my bow in hand and headed up the mountain the following morning. Everything seemed back on track now. There was no question that I felt better...and there were still four days of the season left.

The sky was just beginning to orange above the peaks as I slid the pack off my shoulders and began to fumble about in the dark with the tent. Usually I can get it set up in 15 minutes or so, even in the dark. But I'd not been very organized when I packed everything up yesterday. In fact, I'd been very disorganized. By the time the tent was up and the sleeping bag had been unfurled inside and my day pack set out and the Kelty stowed, it was completely daylight. It was all right though—there wasn't any way I could have gotten to where I intended to go by daylight, even if I hadn't set up camp. I finally set out across the mountain. Finding sheep didn't seem as important right now as did the feeling of being well.

I headed north along the ridgetop and two miles later swung east toward Sheep Mountain (sounds fictitious, but it's not). I'd seen rams on the backside before the season opened and I had a feeling that no one had even been near there since. It was a long walk and then a steep climb. If I found the rams there it might be best to move everything closer. Water might be a problem though. I'd not found any when I was there in July. There were some scattered snow patches here and there, remnants of last week's early snow, but probably not enough for any kind of comfort. Well, we'd just have to see.

By 11:00 I was sitting just below the skyline on the east side of the mountain looking down into a long, narrow, rockstrewn basin that was as rough as this country ever gets. Further to the north the basin ended against a long ridge that connected the east and west portions of the mountain. There was a small bowl back to the west that looked as much like natural sheep pasture as anything I'd ever seen. I'd found the rams here in July. To the east the long ridge formed a box canyon that was a jumble of boulders as large as houses. Escape country, I figured.

I'd already spent an hour glassing the basin and the box canyon—or as much of it as I could see from this angle. Nothing but one very small mule deer buck and he'd seen me slip over the skyline and had moved down into the trees at the south end of the basin. It sure looked like good sheep country. And it sure looked remote. I moved back over the skyline and went a half mile north to the end of the basin before slipping back again to the east side. I try never to move about in the open where I expect to see sheep. A sheep's eyesight is legendary. I wouldn't guess at how far away they can spot skylined or moving objects. Several miles, I'm sure. If sheep spot you, they may well lay themselves right where they are and not move a muscle until you're out of sight. And then they'll be up and gone...probably into rougher, more remote country, not to be seen again for four or five days. I didn't have that kind of time to waste.

I glassed and scoped every inch of the rocky basin across and below me. I was looking almost straight down on the bowl where I'd seen the rams in July.

Nothing was moving. I decided to have my lunch and wait around for a while before I moved on. Sheep are often up and feeding around noontime. Usually they don't move far from their bed...sometimes they are up for only a few minutes, sometimes for an hour or so. I continued glassing as I ate lunch. It felt good sitting in the sun.

By 2:00 p.m. I decided to move further north and have a look at the other side of the long, connecting ridge. As I walked north I noticed that directly below where I'd eaten lunch the mountain side sloped away and then fell into a series of ledges and undercuts that weren't visible from where I sat. It was a long way down to where I'd be able to see over and into them, but it seemed foolish not to at least look. The mountain fell away sharply and then became a narrow ridge before it dropped into the ledges and undercuts. I climbed down about 400 yards before I could see over the side. I sat and glassed into as much as I could see. Most of the undercuts could only be thoroughly seen from the other side of the basin. I could see nothing from here. As I stood to go back up the mountain a piece of sheep horn and a nose came out and into view from an undercut about 100 yards below me. It was only visible for a moment and then it was gone. I jumped back away from the edge. I didn't think I'd been seen. At least the part of the ram I'd seen hadn't been looking my way.

Grabbing my bow I moved quickly down the ridge, being careful to stay well back from the edge. When I figured I'd gone 75 yards or so, I took off my pack and crawled to the edge to look over. I couldn't see anything. But then, from this new position, I couldn't be sure just where I'd seen the ram's horn. I kept crawling slowly forward trying to see back under the ridge.

A movement to my left, which was back up the mountain, caught my eye. Not 50 yards away, facing away from me, stood a ram. Its head was down, feeding. I quickly rolled back away from the edge and out of sight. All I knew for sure was that it was a ram—there had been no time to see anything else.

Now what? There was one ram above me and one presumably below me. I didn't really know if either was shootable. Crawling back to the center of the ridge, I climbed back up the mountain for a better look. At about the spot from which I'd originally seen the ram's horn appear, I crawled out to the edge and looked down. There was a very dark ram bedded on top of a huge boulder about 150 yards below me, looking out at the basin below. He had not been there before. There was no sign of the feeding ram. Could this possibly be the same ram?

Moving back from the edge, I went down the ridge again. This time I eased to a place I thought to be just above the ram on the boulder. Again I crawled to the edge and peeked over. This time I was watching uphill to my left also. The feeding ram was not visible. The one on the rock was still there, now

about 40 or 50 yards away.

The ridge I was on curved away from the ram further down, so moving wasn't going to get me much closer than I was. This was too far for my taste. And besides, I couldn't see enough of the ram to decide if I was interested in taking a shot. I wish I knew where the other ram was...or if there even was another ram.

In order to get closer I'd have to go completely over the edge and then I'd be totally in the open. I didn't think it could be done. I had to get back up the mountain for another look. Crawling back from the edge I again climbed back up the mountain for a better view. Still only one ram. And it didn't look

Photo by Judd Cooney

as though I could get any closer than I'd been. It was really hard to tell much about him from the way he was bedded. I'd just have to get close and wait for him to move later in the day. The wind would likely continue blowing up the mountain until just before sunset.

Back down the ridge I went. Out to the edge I crawled. He was gone. Damn! I was sure he hadn't smelled me. Maybe he'd seen me...or heard me. But I didn't think so. He must have simply gotten up to feed and moved around the point of the ridge to his right. If he'd gone to the left, he'd be visible. Jerking off my pack, I put an arrow on the string and started cautiously, but quickly, edging down the ridge.

I'd only gone a short distance when the backs of two sheep with their heads down feeding came into view 60 to 100 yards below me. I dropped to the ground instinctively. There was absolutely no cover between us. It was pure luck that both had their heads down when I spotted them. I could only think of one thing to do. Lying on my back, I placed my bow, with an arrow on the string, across my thighs. I laid myself back with my head flat on the ground and began inching slowly down the mountain feet first. Hell, I wasn't even sure if I wanted to shoot at either of them. But I figured with my head back on the ground, if I could get to where I could see the animal out of the top of my eyes I'd be close enough to sit up, make a decision and shoot...if I decided to.

I'm not sure how long it took, but it seemed like a long time before I saw the very top of a set of sheep horns appear above the grass. As I raised slowly to a sitting position, both rams were looking at me. They were both three-quarter curls.

I wasn't aware of actually saying to myself, "Do it." But from my sitting position I came to full draw with the bow canted parallel to the ground and shot the biggest of the two through the chest.

Both rams whirled and were out of sight down the mountain in a half second. I leaped to my feet and began running toward the edge to try and keep them in sight, but I lost my footing and went crashing headlong down the mountain. My new bow hit with a clatter on a large rock and went skidding and bouncing down the mountain. What a way to field test a bow! Regaining my footing, and my bow, I ran to a point where I could see the entire valley below. Nothing. That's what I get for chasing after a hit animal. Rookie!

I began criss-crossing the mountain looking for blood but found nothing. I admonished myself for trying to start in the middle and began climbing back up toward where I actually shot the animal. I'd shot enough animals to know that my arrow had hit exactly where it should, but there is always that gnawing doubt until you find the animal.

As I climbed back up toward my pack I came to a place where I could see off the north side of the ridge again. I could see him from there, piled up in the rocks some 200 yards below me. Instead of going straight down the mountain as I assumed he would, he circled back around the end of the ridge and looked to have been headed for the box canyon. I stood for a long time looking down there at him. I wanted to yell at the top of my voice but the sound caught in my throat. Something in me wanted to do it but something else said the dignity of the animal and the moment would be ruined. Lord, after all these years, and there lay the end of it.

I started down toward him and then I stopped. I thought about this being the only time I would ever get to do this—only once in a lifetime. I wanted it to last. I walked down the slope a little and then I sat for a while and looked at him and at the mountains for awhile. I felt sorry for everyone who had never hunted something for seven years before they were finally successful. And I felt sorry for me because I wouldn't ever feel this way again.

Reprinted from **Bowhunter Magazine**, June/July 1982

The author and his trophy.

13

Photo by Judd Cooney

''Nothing had come easy for Bob and me on this trip.''

The Water Test

After 15 days of inspecting every likely—and unlikely—piece of moose habitat in British Columbia, my mind refused to believe the rumor started by my eyes. But there they were again and there was no doubting it. I saw a huge set of moose horns, bobbing and dipping up and down in the willow brush. Then they were gone.

Now every man in the boat had seen it while Bob and I scrambled after our binoculars, each wanting to be the first to proclaim his qualifications. Bill Love, like all good crusty guides, pronounced the beast monstrous without ever taking his hand off the tiller. He had instinctively cut the outboard's drone to a murmur as he began easing the craft at an angle across the lake.

It was good to be seeing game, even if we were all soaking wet and half frozen from being in the rain all day, as one often is in the Canadian wilderness. Wading through neck-high willows had completed the job of soaking our woolens through to the skin.

Now we could see a second set of moose horns; they looked smaller than the others. There were two moose, taking their evening meal less than 50 yards off the shoreline, an area we had glassed several times. The biggest spread had to be at least 60 inches, with his sidekick 45 to 50 inches.

I found myself wishing it were earlier in the day and wishing harder than ever that the rain would stop. After four days of nothing but a continuous cold rain, my sinuses had gone down for the third time and, all day long, had been signaling me of their disapproval. Moreover, I was far from sure that my cold, stiff muscles could be depended on to wrestle my bow to full draw.

Bob and I had been thinking of nothing but a warm tent and a cup of brew as we walked in silence for the last hour down the mountain and back to our boat, but now I was trying hard to steer myself back into a hunting frame of mind. Since Bob had already taken his moose, this was to be my show. I wished that I could talk my moose into staying put until morning—when I would feel more like a predator and less like a drowned rat.

Now we were almost across the lake and nearing a point some 800 yards below the moose. The wind was in the right direction and steady and if the moose had sighted us as we quietly negotiated the lake they had given us no sign. I began stripping off my outer jacket and slipped on my arm guard and glove. A couple of tugs on my bow convinced me that my adrenalin was coming to the rescue of my stiff muscles. The 77-pound bow felt just right for a record Canadian moose. I thought for a second about leaving my wool jacket on, but discarded the idea. Just then the boat bumped against rocks as it nosed into the shore.

Bill and I hopped over the bow of the boat, glanced back at the two huddled figures in it—to accept their silent "good lucks"—and headed up the bank. It was growing dark fast.

Once on top of the bank we found a trail that seemed to lead in the direction of the moose we had seen; however, I was not able to pick them up with my binoculars. There seemed to be three or four slight rises, all of them covered with thick six-foot willow brush between us and our quarry. But, without seeing the moose, everything else seemed to be just right. The stiff wind, whipping down the lake and hitting us in the face, blew in our favor. As we moved quickly down the trail I was thinking that this all seemed a bit too easy. The fast approaching darkness was our only concern.

Nothing had come easy for Bob and me on this trip. We found game very scarce even though on some days we covered up to 30 miles with our guides. Huge valleys and basins that always produced trophy heads for Bill's clients now lay hushed and unpopulated. Wolf tracks were everywhere. On two occasions we had seen huge packs loping across the tundra in that ground-eating gait of theirs, their noses intent on something warm. The few other animals which we did see were terribly skittish and rarely took a second look at anything they suspected of being unfriendly. It seemed that the wolves had taught them to "run now and ask questions later." But some luck had been with us. I had taken a caribou on the eleventh day and Bob had gotten a moose a few days later. However, those had been our only stalks or shots.

After 15 minutes of walking, Bill and I could see the very top of the smaller moose's rack; our trail had taken us to within 100 yards of the feeding animals. Now we were faced with a problem I had been wrestling with ever since we left the boat. Which moose do we tackle? By this time the smaller one was rather close while the big one was some 60 to 80 yards beyond his partner. The wind was still in our favor but there simply wasn't time for us to make as big a circle as we needed to get around the smaller moose and next to the big one. Of course, I wanted the big one.

Bill and I squatted below the moose's line of vision as, in whispered tones, we tried to arrive at a hurried decision. The fact was, whatever decision was made, I wanted only one result—that biggest bull looking down at me from above my fireplace. We decided to try circling inland and coming in beyond the smaller moose, but if we did it wrong he would scent us and go crashing off, taking the big bugger with him. We banked on the wind quartering enough to make our strategy work and began our circle. Halfway around, the breeze on the back of our necks told us we had been caught in an eddy. We quickly backed out.

When we returned to our circle's starting point, I was surprised to find that the moose were still feeding. I was beginning to worry. We couldn't circle in the opposite direction—the lake was there. What had looked like a rather simple stalk was now turning out altogether in the moose's favor. Then I switched targets: with darkness closing in, with only two days of hunting left and these being the only two bull moose I had seen or would be likely to see, I elected to take the smaller of the two home with me.

He was about 60 yards away now, feeding on the same trail we were on and facing our way. Moving any further down the trail wouldn't work and darkness would overtake us if we tried to wait. Like most of us, I have an intense aversion to taking a dip in real cold water, but there was no other choice. By way of the lake lay my last chance to take a trophy home.

Bill waited by the trail as I slipped into the edge of the lake to finish my stalk. I could at least make a silent approach. The water, fortunately, was below my boot tops. It was better than I had imagined. It was a piece of cake. I congratulated myself for choosing this easy route; the next moment I was up to my waist in the icy water. My foot had slipped on the slick rock bottom. As I got to my feet I was almost afraid to look—surely the bulls had heard my splash and my bow clattering on the rocky shore as it went flying from my grasp. How uncoordinated can one get?

I thank the gods of the hunt for chewy, crunch willow: both of the moose were still up to their ears in dinner. The water slapping the rocks had also helped to muffle the noise I made.

Hard as it was to disregard the cold water that soaked me from my waist down and filled my boots, I resumed my stalk but I was now more careful where I placed my feet. Moving on, I was just squatting down to duck an overhanging bush when the smaller of the two bulls turned toward the lake and walked directly at me. I froze in my hunched position as he chose the willow in front of me to continue his feeding. I tried to disappear by sinking to my knees in the icy water. The moose raised his massive head for a mouthful and looked directly at me. He continued looking at me as he chomped away. And he was less than 20 feet from me. I expected at any instant to see him stiffen up—a sign that he recognized an enemy. But he continued stripping the bush, limbs and all, sounding like a giant ice crusher in low gear.

I felt panic setting in as he continued working toward me, picking a mouthful first here and then there. It was obvious that I was pinned down—too close to move without being detected and directly in front of the grazing animal's eyes. I couldn't believe that he was looking right through me and yet not seeing me at all—at 20 feet. This had to be

Photo by Judd Cooney

''I wanted only one result—that biggest bull looking down at me from above my fireplace.''

the high water mark of bowhunting boners—I could hear his stomach growling!

Finally he was two feet off the water's edge and eight to 10 feet in front of me. A frontal shot looked impossible; besides I don't like them. But waiting for a broadside as he passed would put him within three feet of me. The wind was still good, but a hurricane couldn't prevent detection at three feet.

Then it occurred to me that if I failed to shoot him at once, he would either see me, smell me or step on me before another minute ticked by. And the darkness was getting thicker. Besides, the freezing water was beginning to numb my whole body. I worried, wondering if my fingers could hold the string if I tried to release an arrow.

I felt that any movement now on my part was sure to be detected, but something had to be done. Slowly, ever so slowly, I extended my bow arm straight up toward the bull, which was probably four feet above me, and canted my bow almost level to clear the water. My moose failed to detect any movement on my part even though he was looking straight at me.

I decided to take him when he next raised his head for a jawful of the bush above him. His neck would be fully extended and hopefully an arrow at the junction of neck and brisket would penetrate far enough to do the trick. There was the stretch. I felt a feather brush my cheek and then the arrow was away and the sound of my bow and the surprised grunt of the bull blended as the arrow hit exactly where I had aimed.

With a deafening bellow he came falling through the bush to crash into the water on his knees at my feet. A shower of water—his splash— almost drowned me, but I was unable to feel a thing. I was frozen to the spot—figuratively and most literally— as the bull rose out of the water like a monster from a Japanese late movie. He turned and took about three steps as he clambered out of the water onto the bank. He stood quietly and took a look around. I snapped out of my trance when it flashed through my mind that he might be looking for me. Just as

I reached for another arrow his hind legs collapsed and he fell off the embankment and back into the water. The crash of his massive horns resounded across the rocks. He was dead.

The deadliness of a single arrow never ceases to amaze me. It doesn't seem possible that one arrow, driven by 77 pounds, can stop a 1,500 pound animal in a matter of seconds. Sometimes I smile to myself when people tell me what an advantage rifle hunters have over me, with my primitive weapon. In a way they do have an advantage, but for my money it is only because they can kill from greater distances.

Bill came out of the willows to congratulate me. He had waited about 20 yards away and he was certain when I released my arrow that the bull was standing on me. When we yelled we heard the outboard kick to life and start toward us. He wasn't a monster bull, but he was decently large. A check with the tape was enough to let me know that he would make the records—easy enough. I was pleased with the quick kill and my only disappointment was that I didn't get a chance at the big one.

Bob and Buster arrived in the boat and jumped into the ankle-deep water. They had heard the bellow of the bull when I shot him and they heard his horns clatter on the rocks when he collapsed. They were sure that I had taken the big one and was now the possessor of a new world record.

We would only gut him, we decided, since it was after nine o'clock. In the morning we would come and load up the meat. He lay with his horns in the water so the job of getting him into a boat was made that much easier. We draped my jacket over a bush to discourage any wolves from stopping by for a late snack.

The four of us piled into the boat for the long ride up the lake and supper as soon as we reached camp. The rain had begun falling harder, but it didn't seem so cold. Bob and I huddled onto the bottom of the boat, out of the driving wind. We were lost in our own thoughts about my moose trophy and how good supper was going to taste.

Reprinted from **Bowhunter Magazine**, February/March 1977

The author passes ''The Water Test'' with flying colors.

14

Photo by Judd Cooney

''Most years we'll see at least one really big deer somewhere on the mountain.''

One Season on Pritchard Mountain

It was a strange, different sort of year. Right from the very first. Nothing to worry about, really. But it was different.

First off, I'd never hunted this mountain by myself. And that wasn't a big deal...I mean, not that I was afraid of anything. But back in 1969—that first year I'd moved to Colorado—Bob Pitt had come out from Indiana in August and we'd found this place. Every year since then, come late summer, he and I came here to hunt mule deer.

I'm superstitious about changing things that are good. And this had always been good. It would seem almost sacrilegious to be up here without him. But this year his business wouldn't allow him to leave. So I was mule deer chasing by myself. Then, two days ago the four-wheel drive had gone out of my old green Blazer. Rather than wait for it to be fixed and miss the opening day of the season, I'd said "To heck with it" and sallied forth with only two of the four wheels working. It was rare that you needed four-wheel drive up here anyway. The ranch roads were good and I couldn't remember the last time it had rained enough up here in August to be a problem.

And then on the drive over the mountain, a perfectly good tire had gone flat. The worst part, of course, was having to unload half the truck to get to the spare. But it didn't go that bad and in a half hour I was on the road again.

The mountain belongs to the Pritchard family. Old Tom Pritchard was into his 80s when we first met him. He claimed his father had been running cows up there before Colorado was a state. They're good people. Old Tom's son, Young Tom, runs the place now, along with his boys, Bobby, Ned, Lyle and Dick. The ranch house is located down at the base of the mountain near the little town of Gypsum, which isn't much more than a wide place in the road. There's a grocery and a gas station and a liquor store. The liquor store is owned by the guy who owns the gas station. If you want to wet your whistle you have to walk across the dusty street and ask politely if someone could open up for you. Sometimes they will and sometimes they won't...it depends on how busy they are at the station. And sometimes they won't go if they've just been over there or if they're expecting a customer or an important phone call. The prices are not competitive.

Well, as it turned out, I wasn't going to have the mountain to myself. At least not for the weekend. The Pritchards had planned a family reunion this weekend. And what better place to have it than up there in the old family cabin? Tom said there would be a bunch of them there...probably 30 or 40, counting all the kids. The women were already on top at the cabin, cooking and cleaning up a bit. Most of the year, except for an occasional cowboy who overnights there, the old cabin only sees hunters anymore. A little feminine touch with a broom wouldn't do the place any harm.

Old Tom, Young Tom, Dick and I sat in the shade under the big cottonwoods in front of the ranchhouse, had a cool drink and talked for awhile about the mountain and the deer and the cool drinks and just what effect this earlier bow season was going to have on things. Old Tom reckoned the early season was a mistake by the Fish and Game Department. Old Tom figured **anything** coming out of the Fish and Game Department was a mistake.

When Mrs. Pritchard called everyone to lunch I begged off with a "Gotta be getting on up on top" and a "See you up there tonight" and drove out of the yard. Yeah, they were good people and I knew I was fortunate to know them. I thought some about that as I drove across the dry, dusty sage flat toward the mountain. Mostly I thought about the coming hunt. I wondered how long the reunion would last. More than likely it wouldn't be any one day affair...not if what I knew about the Pritchards held true. Knowing these cowboys, I figured it would be one fine, large night. **Nobody** can party like cowboys.

It's 26 miles from the ranchhouse to the cabin. Given the quality of the roads, it's about a two-and-one-half hour drive. Usually we see a lot of deer on the way in, but it was the middle of the day and I only saw a single doe. One year we drove up right at dark. We must have seen 200 deer after we hit the top. One was a real whopper. Bob and I both came back to the area during the week looking for him but we never saw him again. Bob guessed he'd go up around 180 or 185 Pope and Young points. There aren't a lot of deer that size around anywhere. Most years we'll see at least one really big deer somewhere on the mountain. Normally we'll see a lot of decent bucks, maybe a half dozen of them will be over 155 inches...which is getting into the respectable deer category. It's a good place. We've shot a lot of good deer here. More importantly, perhaps, there have been a lot of good times here. This was going to be my 12th or 13th

year walking the ridges on this old mountain. She's become like a good wife to me...a real pleasure and a real friend.

The girls came to the door and waved as I drove in on the little knoll above the cabin. There's a little flat spot there between the cabin and the heavy stand of aspen on the hillside that stays in the shade most of the day. We'd set up camp there before. I walked down to the cabin and said "Hello" before I started setting up camp. "Hello" took longer than I'd planned and by the time I had the tent up the sun was already dropping into the afternoon sky. I was glad I'd remembered my tent, even though it was the small one. Most years we stay in the cabin and a tent and stove and outdoor cooking paraphernalia are only along "just in case." I'd rather be outside anyway. The cabin is nice, especially the big cooking stove. And it is nice and cool and dark inside during the heat of the day. But it is too big for just one person. It always seems to me that sleeping on the ground, outside in a tent, allows you to be part of the outdoors...and that's important when I'm hunting. In a man-made structure...a cabin, a house...you're separated from the outdoors...glass windows and doors and walls do that. A tent allows you to wrap the outdoors around you...you're in the middle of it all. A house serves to protect you, to insulate you from the outdoors.

I was still getting organized when the steady parade of Ford 4x4s loaded with kids and red and white plastic coolers began wheeling into the cabin yard. The cowboys were arriving. Trying to ignore the steady "plomp, plomp, plomp" of opening and closing cooler lids, I worked as fast as I could, knowing that once I stopped and joined the festivities...and it would be expected that I do that...it would be the end of my hunting preparations. I laid out everything I'd need in the morning...pants, shirt, T-shirt. I put my belt into the pants, loaded the pockets with all the strange things that bowhunters carry and set my Bean Hunting Shoes side by side, with appropriate socks laid on top. Almost forgot the hat...it goes right on top of the socks. I'd already assembled the new prototype Bighorn Takedown, attached the new bow quiver loaded with razor sharp Black Diamonds and hung the whole thing in the tree by the cooking table. I was kind of excited about the new bow...testing it, shooting it and banging it around. That's the best part of building bows...getting to test them in the woods. I hadn't shot it as much as I should have. But by the end of tomorrow I would have probably shot it at least 500 more times. Everything was ready. All I'd have to do in the morning was pull everything on and grab my bow...30 seconds at the most, I figured. I zipped the tent and started down toward the cabin. Looked like a little rainstorm might be blowing in from the west.

Well, I was right about the cowboys. The family reunion roared and rolled and continued to gather speed all night. I slipped away during the fourth telling of the great wreck that had taken place one night last spring when Lyle and Ned had raced off the mountain on a bet about whether a Ford would outrun a Chevy. I thought then that one day I ought to write a book about these guys. Nobody would believe I hadn't made it up...

It was a short night...as I'd figured it would be. I pulled on my clothes and crawled out of the tent. I could hear someone coughing...sort of...and when I looked down toward the cabin I could see someone tall, but bent over, with their hands on their knees. I grabbed my bow, tossed it in the back and jumped in the Blazer. I was still pretty groggy from lack of sleep but as soon as I let out the clutch I could tell I had a flat tire...a flat, flat, flat, **flat**, flat tire. *Lord, don't do this to me on opening morning...I deserve better treatment than this, Lord.*

I shut off the engine, leaped out, dropped the tailgate and grabbed the spare. It took a full 15 seconds for the shock to wear off...how very absolutely, totally stupid can you be? *No!* I groaned. I ***could not*** have done that!

I had not gotten my spare repaired after yesterday's flat tire. I've probably had three flats in my entire life and it just had not occurred to me. Now here I was...opening morning of Colorado's mule deer season...26 miles from the nearest house...probably 40 miles from the nearest place to have a tire patched. I thought about it for about another 17 seconds, then I grabbed my bow and set

out at a fast pace up the hill behind the cabin toward the nearest, best place for mule deer that I could think of. It wasn't what I'd had in mind, but it was better than the alternatives.

It wasn't a very good morning. Tire problems aside, the wind was swirling badly and everytime I took a step, if I didn't crack a stick I flushed a half dozen does. I didn't see a decent buck. By 10:00 I was on my way back to camp and my flat tires.

Everyone in the cabin was up and dressed. I'd never seen so many people in one room. They must have slept eight to a bed. There were a few slow movers but mostly everyone was grinning. They kidded me a bit about being a greenhorn and a city boy and offered some tongue-in-cheek advice on always carrying a spare tire when going to the mountains. I tried to laugh with them. Ned said he'd take me and my two flat tires down for repair after he'd had some breakfast. We ended up having to go most of the way to Grand Junction. The guy who owned the garage in Gypsum said he was expecting a lot of liquor store business that day and didn't want to start into a big project like patching two tires...but, if we wanted to leave them...

That night I went to the cabin and had dinner with all four generations of Pritchards. I tried to keep my wits about me because I planned to give the muleys what for on Sunday. But someplace in there I decided that staying for the after dinner show was the thing to do. Cowboy logic is catching, I guess. During the evening they said I danced with Ned's eight-year-old daughter...and there wasn't a band...and I remember Ned's brother-in-law, Steve, holding a Coleman® lantern while I demonstrated the basics of instinctive bowshooting to 40 people...30 of which had never seen anyone ever shoot a bow and wouldn't have known what I was even doing if I hadn't told them. Another fine, large night.

Sunday morning came earlier than I wanted it to. It was a foggy, drizzly morning with the sky right down on the ground. Too muggy for woolens. And rain suits, as always, would be too noisy. Whatever I wore would be soaked in 10 minutes, so I pulled on yesterday's cotton camo and set out...again on foot...seeing as how my Blazer's four-wheel drive was inoperable and the roads were undoubtedly impassable in two-wheel drive. It may have been the most perfect stalking weather I've ever seen. The rain was a mist...almost a fog. I felt like a ghost slipping through it...never making even the slightest sound. I've read that deer...and, I guess, elk...do not see well in this sort of weather. Something to do with their not being able to keep the rain out of their eyes...that they end up with a constant film of water over their eyes. I've never been sure whether that was true or not but two different bucks walked within feet of me, looked right at me and never knew I was around. A herd of seven cow elk and their calves fed up to—and then around—me and never raised an eyebrow. And I shot four blue grouse on the ground when they wouldn't fly and never felt a twinge of conscience. It was a fine, large morning. By 10:00 the rain stopped and the clouds raised a bit but you could tell it would rain again before the day was over.

The Pritchard family started pulling their things together right after lunch. Everyone wanted to get down through the switchbacks while the ground was drying out and before it started raining again. Bob and I drove off once while it was raining; I said then I'd never do it again. When you add a tea cup of water, the dirt up here turns the consistency of grease. Vehicles slide down hills in this mud...from their own weight. I sat on the front bumper of Old Tom's pickup and drank coffee with him and watched everyone breaking camp. Each woman gathered her family's stuff together and set it in a place; then her husband carried it out and loaded it. Each generation of the family did it the same way. I wondered if there was some sort of premarital agreement that the men took no part in the gathering and the women took no part in the loading. By 4:00 I had the mountain to myself.

About two hours before dark I drove out west toward the points to look around a little. The rain storm the sky had been promising just sat there in the form of black clouds and waited. It was probably waiting for me to get a little farther from camp before it opened up. I did a lot of glassing until dark, but only saw one decent buck and he was on the opposite mesa a mile away across the valley. Out near the points are where we usually find the big

deer on this mountain. While I call this place "a mountain," it isn't what one would normally think of as a mountain, with timberlines and rocky pinnacles and such. "The mountain" is really a huge, flat-topped mesa that sits 2,500 feet above everything else. All around the edge of the mesa are long points of land that may be half a mile long and sometimes not over a few hundred yards wide...although they may be much longer and wider. The biggest bucks seem to prefer these isolated points because they can easily escape over the edges into the cliffs below.

The next morning I drove east and slipped into a patch of quakies I knew. The trees grew right up the edge of one of the points and below the oak brush was thick enough to hide a tank. Bob shot the biggest non-typical to ever come off this mountain as it came up out of the brush a couple of years ago. We didn't weigh it but it was the biggest bodied deer I've ever seen. I tried to conjure up his twin as I alternately slipped and stood and slipped and stood. But there was only a doe and her twin fawns there. After she got around behind me, she took her children crashing back down through the oak brush, warning anything else that might have any interest in coming this way. I've always wanted to say, "Hey, listen, lady...I'm not going to shoot you...I could you know, but I'm not going to. But you've got to promise that you'll walk quietly and not tell another soul about me being here."

At about 8:30 the sky opened up and it started raining, softly at first and then harder and harder. After another half hour I gave it up and started back to the Blazer. I was sure I'd never make it up the one hill close to camp. Sometimes 4x4 pickups without any weight in the back had trouble there. The Blazer didn't get halfway up before it began spinning and sliding helplessly. I left it there and walked back to camp. Like I said, this was a different year. Most years, we've prayed for rain while we were hunting. Every year, except this one, my 4x4 Blazer would have loved to tackle that hill...but this year I'd come without four-wheel drive and naturally it was going to rain for the whole bloody season.

It rained on and off for the next three days. I'd

Photo by Judd Cooney

"I sure spooked a lot of deer in those next few days."

get up long before daylight and with a candy bar in my pocket I'd set off for the day on foot. A couple of times it hailed so hard that it hurt when it hit you. I tried a couple of times to get the Blazer up the hill with no luck. I did manage to get it out of the middle of the road and back down to a level place. The hunting wasn't going well. I couldn't get to the places I needed to be.

And then the sun came out. Within four hours you couldn't have stuck a pickax in the road bed. That's the way it is in Colorado. On Friday the thermometer on the cabin said it was 91 degrees at 1:30 in the afternoon. I started seeing a few more deer now that I could cover more ground. One morning I got to within 35 yards of a nice buck feeding in a sage park. But he saw me when I tried to get closer and he didn't wait around. That same afternoon right at dark I watched two bucks feed out of a dense clump of serviceberry below me and cross over to the other side of the valley before I lost them in the dark. I'd have shot one of them, if given the chance. I slip-hunted the area they were headed into the next morning, but I didn't see them. It started getting so hot during midday that the deer weren't moving until right at dark. And a couple of times I ran into deer already bedded down an hour after daylight.

During the middle of the day I spent a lot of time shooting my bow. I was shooting the new prototype takedown pretty good now and I felt sure that any deer that let me get close was in a heap of trouble. One of the real enjoyable parts of mule deer and elk hunting is that the weather and the type of hunting allow for lots of time for shooting your bow. On a two week mule deer hunt I might well shoot 1,500 to 2,500 arrows. I'd never been a big bow quiver fan. Every one I'd ever tried rattled and made all kinds of noise. For years I'd used a St. Charles-type back quiver. But this new bow quiver was certainly changing my mind. It was completely quiet and I was beginning to think that the added weight was improving my shooting. You sure couldn't deny the convenience of the thing while you were slipping around in the brush.

Time was getting a little short so I decided to start hunting during the heat of the day. I knew that it's best to still-hunt while deer are on their feet moving around. Your chances of seeing them are greater and their chances of seeing you are reduced. No question about it. But there was really nothing to lose...I couldn't hunt forever. I knew a lot of places where I could always find deer bedded; the problem was the cover was usually so thick you had to step on deer to see them. Of course, that wasn't the real problem...the real problem was that it was so thick they heard you coming a long time before you were close enough to step on them. I sure spooked a lot of deer in those next few days. Only a couple of times was I able to get fairly close to a good buck. Both times I saw them after they'd bolted out of cover.

There is one particular point where, every year, big deer like to lay during the middle of the day. It is a fairly sparse and open patch of oak brush, not over 35 yards wide and 75 yards long...but there are open hillsides on each side and deer could see everything in front and, because of the prevailing wind, smell everything from their rear. It was a good place for them. I'd been trying to catch them going into or going out of it all week. Finally, in desperation, I crawled 150 yards across the barren hillside under the midday sun, pushing my bow ahead of me. In truth, I wasn't even sure there was a deer bedded there this day...although I'd seen them come into it several times this hunt. I was soaking wet with sweat and must have had a hundred sharp things sticking in as many places when I finally bellied into the edge of the brush. Now that I was in position, there was some question as to just what I was going to do. I couldn't stand up. If there was a deer bedded here, I was likely within 30 yards of him.

Keeping my head as low as possible, I got my knees under me and tried to look around. The first thing I saw was a deer bedded just down the hill in front of me. His head, with a huge set of antlers atop it, was in the process of turning completely around looking straight back up the hill at me. It might have been 12 or 15 yards. I shot very quickly and heard a nice solid sound; then the deer crashed away through the brush. It took one-half second to get to where he had been bedded...and another 15 minutes to get the arrow out of the trunk of the little oak bush. It was just slightly bigger than my thumb and as near as I could tell probably covered no more than 1/50th of that buck's vitals. It just wasn't his time to die...that's all I could figure...because the chances of that little bush saving his life had to be close to zero. He was a good buck. No way of knowing how good, but he looked over 160 to me...but it happened too fast to know really. Well...fool that I am, I felt encouraged by my having gotten in on the big bugger. I could do it again...on another big one...I knew I could.

The next morning I jumped two big boys out of a jumbled pile of downed timber near the top of a ridge. They'd been resting where they could watch me as I slipped up an old cow trail and hadn't moved until they were sure I was coming their way. I ran to the top of the ridge in time to see them disappear into the top of a quakie patch on the other side. I remembered that patch of timber. We'd named it "the bowl" because it was almost completely round and was straight up on the sides. For several years Bob and I had seen a lot of deer there. We hadn't hunted much in there for awhile. Jordan Ray, who'd come with us one year, had shot a nice 3x4 there. I remembered we had a devil of a time getting it out. I sat and watched the place for a long time. They didn't come out where I could see them but they could have gone out one place in the bottom or gone back over the ridge at another place I couldn't see. I had a feeling they'd stayed there. Maybe I'd just pay them a little visit later in the day.

I'd quit looking at the thermometer the last few days. It just made me hotter to put a number to it. It was hot...that was for sure. I shot a few arrows and lay myself down in the shade for awhile. Tomorrow would have to be my last day. Maybe I could get back for another weekend if I didn't score this afternoon or tomorrow morning.

At 1:00 I drove as close to "the bowl" as I could and then climbed up above it and sat and tried to figure out the best way to still-hunt it considering the wind and where I thought deer might be bedded. It really wasn't all that big a place. I remembered that if you came in all the way at the bottom you'd immediately be seen by anything

bedded on the steep sides. I decided the best way was to drop off the back of this ridge, swing around the point in the oak brush and then come straight around through the middle of some trees, ight about where it really got steep. That way I'd be working across the wind and I should be in under everything's line of sight. It must have been close to 2:30 or 3:00 by the time I worked my way around and into position to begin seriously inching through the bowl. Compared to the open ridgetop, it felt like there was an air conditioner going in here. The deer liked it, too...there were beds everywhere. I moved slowly forward, sure I was going to see antlers sticking out of the high grass at any moment. As I moved forward, it began getting steeper and steeper. In a couple of places a shot at a deer would have been almost straight up. This was the hottest-looking place I'd seen this year.

Reminding myself that tomorrow was the last day, I moved slowly, carefully and then stood looking longer than I normally do before moving again. I don't normally still-hunt with an arrow nocked but I was sure something was going to happen soon and I wanted to be ready. Everything was perfect. I was thinking about that as I squatted to pass under a limb and my binoculars swung forward and "clanked" against my bow. Leaning back against the tree, I stood watching everything I could without moving for several minutes. Nothing. I think my foot was already starting to move forward when straight above me a high pair of antlers started inching up and up into view. I was already starting my draw as the head and then the brisket materialized. My elbow hit the tree trunk I was leaning against as I neared full draw. I remember leaning out a bit to clear and then shooting. The arrow disappeared about where I thought it should. The buck seemed to whirl a little to my left, then stood partially behind a tree trunk looking back up toward the top of the ridge, seemingly ignoring me. There was already another arrow on the string but I hesitated about shooting again. Then he disappeared. Climbing quietly toward where I'd last seen him, I was unsure what I might find. The bed he'd been laying in was obvious. Nothing else was, however...no arrow, no blood, no hair. There was a sound, and when I

The satisfying result of one season's hunt on Pritchard Mountain.

looked up the buck was 25 yards above me, stumbling and weaving down toward me. I'm not sure, but I think I just stood there, watching as he came. Then his front legs gave out and he went down and was dead before he'd stopped sliding.

If it were possible, by some mystical power, to be turned into the world's greatest writer, I wonder if I would be able to clearly write down the feelings, the thoughts that are there, in me, at that very first moment when I look down at a big game animal I just killed. Once, maybe twice, I remember feeling victorious. Mostly, it's a feeling of complete calmness...and that isn't it either. I'll have to wait for the mystical writing powers, I think...

The arrow had taken him at the base of the brisket, almost between the front legs, and had gone up and out of him just behind the top of the shoulders along the backbone. The shot had been almost straight up. He wasn't one of the big deer I'd pushed in here this morning but he was a nice deer. The rear points on the back were over 17 inches long and that had really made him look monstrous from down below. I was pleased.

Getting him out of there was going to be a problem. It would be physically impossible to drag him uphill and going downhill just put us farther from the road. There was nothing to do but to quarter him out and pack him out piece by piece. I started the climb up the side of the bowl toward the Blazer and a packframe.

Yeah, it was a weird, different sort of mule deer hunt for me. I sort of felt like I'd pulled off some sort of miracle...family reunions, rain, flat tires, heat, mud and just ordinary bad luck...plain old deer hunting might never be the same again. But all that stuff just made it taste better. It had been just perfect...and maybe after dark I'd build myself a big fire up there on the knoll in front of the tent and stare into it for awhile...

Reprinted from **Bowhunter Magazine**, December/January 1987